All About STEAM COOKING

All About STEAM COOKING

Carol Truax

illustrated by Lauren Jarrett

Doubleday & Company, Inc., Garden City, New York
1981

DESIGNED BY LAURENCE ALEXANDER

ISBN: 0-385-15548-4
Library of Congress Catalog Card Number 79–6878
Copyright © 1981 by Carol Truax

Contents

Recipes designated with an asterisk (*) may be found by consulting the Index.

All About STEAM COOKING

Introduction

IN PRAISE OF STEAM COOKING

Do you remember?—steamed clams to begin the shore dinner, steamed Boston brown bread for Saturday-night supper, steamed plum pudding crowning the Christmas feast—festive days, festive eating!

And festive eating is what comes out of your steamer today: *Mussels Marinière,* Goose in Red Wine, Veal Paprikash, Chestnut Chocolate Pudding. Steam it and eat it!

Steam cooking is supposed to have originated thousands of years ago in the Stone Age. Steaming food wrapped in banana or ti leaves has been the custom from time immemorial wherever these leaves grow. Hawaii still welcomes you with a luau, a kind of Stone Age feast. In the ancient manner, a hole is dug in the ground and lined with stones, and then a fire is built in it to heat the stones. After a time the coals are raked out, and a suckling pig is put in and covered with branches and leaves, with some hot stones to make steam. Finally, the cooked pig comes out in a cloud of fragrant steam, and the feasting begins.

Steam cooking is no longer limited to holes in the ground, nor to primitive places that still remember the Stone Age. It is spreading everywhere, as it should. *Vapeur* (steam) in France produces many dishes that fit well into the popular *cuisine minceur,* the *nouvelle cuisine,* so appealing to the French figure and palate, for instance *Poulette en Papillote* and *Coq au Vin.* The Germans love their *Huhn in Bier.* The Italians fancy their *Bollito Misto* and the delicious *Vitello Tonnato,* which is much better steamed than cooked in deep water. Alsace produces a tasty *Choucroute Garnie.* In North Africa, especially in Algeria and Morocco, everyone, native and foreign, eats the national dish, *Couscous.* Very few can resist Spanish *Paella.* The Irish originated Irish Stew, which, being a white lamb stew, is best cooked in a steamer. The Scotch cook their superb salmon with steam. In the Orient steaming is one of the most popular ways of cooking; no kitchen in China is without a one-, two-, three-or-more tiered steamer, in which they cook *pao-tzu* (dumplings) or *jing-yu* (steamed fish), to name only two out of hundreds of exotic dishes that are cooked with steam in China. Closer to home, the American clambake is a spectacular gustatory occasion, as clams and lobster and corn in the husk are steamed over seaweed. New England has its tasty Boiled Dinner, corned beef and vegetables made succulent by steaming.

Food cooked with steam is so appetizing that you tend to forget that steam cooking has many other advantages.

In steaming, you don't boil the flavor *out,* you steam it *in.* By the same token, you don't boil out the nourishing elements, you steam them in and save them. When you boil your vegetables, the vitamins and minerals go out with the water that you throw away. (Of course you are going to save it for the soup pot, but somehow you never do.)

Those same vegetables are so pretty with their fresh bright colors. Cooked with steam, they stay pretty. They come out of the steamer still bright and decorative, looking as good as they taste, and keeping all the nourishment they began with.

Cuisine vapeur is particularly a *cuisine minceur,* a way of eating that keeps you thin. It is fat-free, low-cholesterol, and low-calorie. You don't need any fat whatever to cook in a steamer, and if fat is present it tends to separate itself with the steam treatment. Food comes out of the steamer virtually fat-free. What you add afterward in the way of a sauce, such as Hollandaise, is strictly between you and your conscience.

Cooking with steam, you can save precious energy, your own and the kind you pay for. Steam in a pressure cooker is energy-efficient, and the three-tiered steamer the Chinese favor makes one burner do the work of three.

Steaming is flavor-making, health-promoting and energy-saving; and you don't have to part with your hard-earned pelf to buy any special equipment if you don't want to. So full steam ahead!

STEAMERS

Steaming is accomplished by cooking over, not in, boiling liquid. The liquid is usually water, sometimes salted, herbed, or combined with broth, wine, or beer.

You don't have to have a special steamer. You can steam the food in foil, or you can adapt any deep utensil with a tight-fitting lid. You prop the food a little above the liquid level. Put large pieces such as chicken or potatoes on an inverted pan or bowl, a strainer, a piece of wire, anything that holds it up. Smaller things are steamed in a bowl or deep platter and usually served in the dish they were cooked in.

You can steam in the oven in a roaster or pot with a rack to hold the fish or meat above the liquid. It must, of course, be covered tight. A roasting pan with its own perforated rack makes a good steamer as long as the rack is held up above the water level and the top fits tight.

A heatproof casserole, soufflé dish, or any pot, round or oval, may be used if the food is kept out of the liquid on a plate or platter held up by custard cups, jar tops, or anything that will support it. Cover it tight. Something as simple as a piece of foil held securely in place by a rubber band will do.

A flat-bottomed colander or one with feet can be put into a large pot with a tight-fitting lid. This makes a fine steamer for many foods if the food is kept above the water.

A French metal strainer has sides of perforated petals, usually with short legs. It can be used for steaming in any saucepan or pot if the lid is tight.

A trivet or wire rack in a roasting pan, high enough to keep the food above the boiling water, is especially good for steaming puddings or large pieces of meat.

A different method of steaming, and a very good one, is cooking in a package of foil or paper. Nothing is more fun at the dinner table than a dish served in a package. The pleasure is threefold. First comes the mysterious package set before you, and the anticipatory pleasure mingled with curiosity sets in. Then you open it, and all the pent-up aroma floods your senses and rouses your appetite for the feast to come.

Nowadays, the family chef cooks it in foil, which is cheap and cheerful. The items to be steamed are folded in securely so none of the delicious juices can escape, for when cooking this way you not only retain all the flavor, but you also often blend flavors and fragrances of the various ingredients and seasonings. Foil packages are usually put into the oven to steam in their own juices, but can also be steamed in a pot on top of the stove. Foil is ideal for steaming, but it takes a little longer, about ten minutes, for the heat to penetrate the metal and start the steaming process.

The original *papillote* so often found in swank restaurants was a parchment bag, and you can still steam food in paper if you want to. Waxed paper or buttered brown paper may be used instead of parchment, since they are more easily available. Don't try plastic; it melts! The one advantage of paper is that you save that extra ten minutes.

While you don't have to buy a flock of new cooking utensils to be a good steam cook, it's nice to add to your kitchen pots, pans, or gadgets from time to time. Here are some suggestions.

A metal steamer with an adjustable perforated rack is available in various sizes. This is the most useful pot for steaming just about anything.

Double boilers may be had with either metal or ceramic tops. They come with two tops, one the usual solid one for dry steaming and the other with a perforated bottom for wet steaming. Very useful.

An asparagus steamer is a high pot, about ten by six or seven inches, with a tight-fitting lid. Such a steamer often has a tray to lift the vegetables out from the top. It is good not only for asparagus but also for broccoli, corn, and other tall vegetables that stand up and are steamed with a little water, about two inches, in the bottom of the pot.

The old-fashioned clam steamers can be used for many things other than clams and lobsters.

New on the market is the stoneware steamer; it has an opening in the center with a trough around it. You put fresh vegetables in the trough, prop it up over boiling water, cover tight, and steam. This suggests using an angel-food or bundt pan or a ring mold the same way.

A French fryer with a basket is fine for steaming; the basket is kept above or often partly submerged in boiling water.

Electric multi-use steamers are on the market, some with a divided layer. These are very satisfactory.

Pressure cookers have been improved in the last twenty years. They combine the advantage of quick cooking with steam cooking. The new ones are easy to regulate, allowing different degrees of pressure or, with the vent open, steam without pressure. Their advantages are not to be neglected. They are especially useful for cooking large pieces of meat. Using pressure, they cut steaming time to one third, which is a great saving of precious energy.

Cooking in wet clay was one of the earliest methods of steaming known to man. As the clay dried, the food was cooked in hot steam. All the flavor and juices stayed in. They still do, but these days we don't have to wrap anything in messy wet clay with our hands. We can buy a clay pot. They are available in various sizes and shapes and are not too expensive.

Food is cooked in clay in a minimum of liquid. It steams and, believe it or not, many foods will brown. However, if you want something crisp, take off the lid for the last ten to fifteen minutes of cooking in a hot oven. There are a few rules. Clay pots are soaked in water for fifteen minutes each time before using. They must always be put into a cold oven. Clay will take very high heat, but not the shock of cold into hot or the opposite. Do not pour cold water into a hot clay pot. If you wish to add moisture while cooking, use a hot liquid. It takes a little longer to cook in clay than in metal and it takes a hotter oven. You start timing fifteen minutes after the pot is put into the oven, since it takes that long for the cold oven to come to the proper temperature. If you have a clay pot, you know how to use it; if you are purchasing one, read and follow the instructions.

There are also special steamers such as the two- or three-tier *couscousière* from Morocco, where the lamb is placed in the bottom, the vegetables in the next tier, and the couscous on top. The pottery ones are traditional; the metal ones are more practical. You don't have to use all three layers. The device is useful for one dish or two as well. This is another steamer that saves energy, as it makes one burner do it all.

Steaming is one of the favorite ways of cooking in China. Many Chinese woks now come equipped with a removable perforated rack to use for steaming. You place pieces of fish, fowl, meat, or vegetables on the rack, put two inches of salted water in the bottom of the wok, cover it tight, and steam until tender. You can steam food in a heatproof bowl or platter on the rack and serve it right in the container it was steamed in. If your wok has no rack, you can place the bowl on an inverted bowl or pan, keeping the bottom of the food container just above the surface of the water. Be sure that the wok is covered tight during the cooking process. At the end, uncover it for a couple of minutes to let the steam disperse so you don't burn your hands.

The ingenious Chinese make great use of stacked, round, woven bamboo layers. These are available by the tier, and you can buy as many as you want. You can use as many as six over the same steam bath—energy-saving again.

Food is served right from the bamboo it was cooked in, which saves *your* energy. A meal in bamboo is easy, and it is a dramatic production as the bamboo trays come to the table in a tall tower and are separated and opened with a flourish, releasing titillating oriental aromas.

Not only does everyone love to cook and eat outdoors, where appetites are rampant, but it is also easy to steam over coals on a small grill such as a hibachi on the terrace, in a fireplace, or even in the kitchen.

Many foods may be steamed in foil on a broiler while a steak grills on another part of the fire. Light the fire far enough ahead to make an even bed of coals; briquettes are very satisfactory and will be ready about half an hour after lighting. You don't need expensive equipment. If you have a built-in outdoor grill or an elaborate one on wheels, use it! If not, a simple portable folding grill will work, or even a piece of perforated metal or mesh placed across stones or bricks will be workable. You *do* need heavy gloves such as padded or asbestos ones. You can pick up a steak with tongs but not a very hot bowl or foil package filled with delicious meat, poultry, fish, vegetables, or fruit. Don't pick corn or potatoes out of the coals without protecting your fingers, but do cook them that way.

With so many kinds of steamers available from France to China and right here at home, purchased or improvised, there is no excuse not to try steaming. Once you try it, you'll never give it up.

HINTS FOR THE STEAM CHEF

Begin timing when the liquid in the cooker starts to boil—after the steam starts. Be sure to cover the steamer *tight*.

Let steam escape before you put your hand in to remove food. Steam is hot!

Check the liquid in the bottom of a steamer. If you cook for a long period of time, you will probably have to replenish the liquid.

You may add salt, herbs, bay leaf, garlic, onion, lemon juice, broth, or wine to the water used for steaming. The liquid can frequently be used for the sauce or gravy.

Do not peek into the steamer too often; you stop the steaming each time. Make up for it by adding several minutes to the steaming time for each time you open the steamer.

Please, always use freshly ground pepper.

All measurements are level.

MENUS

Fish and Seafood

Stuffed Mushrooms with Chicken*
Herbed Bluefish*
New Potatoes*
Okra*
Green Salad
Strawberry Shortcake

Artichokes*
Trout in Paper*
Scalloped Potatoes
Glazed Carrots*
Mocha Ice Cream

Consommé
Fish in Cheesecloth*
Buttered Noodles
Spinach with Cream Cheese*
Blueberry Pudding*

*Celery and Mushrooms**
*Salmon in Aspic**
*Rolls**
Mixed Salad
*Orange Pudding**

*Belgian Endive**
*Seafood Paella**
Green Salad
*Peaches in Wine**

GRILL
Melon
*Fish on a Grill**
*Grill-Roasted Potatoes**
*Green Beans on a Grill**
*Chestnut Chocolate Pudding**

*Asparagus**
*Fillets of Flounder with Tomatoes**
*Cucumbers in Cream Sauce**
*Rice**
*Yeast Buns**
French Pastry

SEAFOOD DINNER
*Steamed Mussels or Oysters**
*Lobster Tails**
Shoestring Potatoes
*Broccoli**
Cucumber Salad
*Rhubarb**

CLAMBAKE
Steamed Clams*
Lobster*
Corn in Husks on a Grill*
Roasted Potatoes
Coleslaw
New England Indian Pudding* with Vanilla Ice Cream

CHINESE
Eggs with Pork*
Sweet and Sour Fish*
Chinese Rice*
Cucumbers
Chinese Cake*

Poultry

Melon
Half Small Broilers en Papillote*
Spoon Bread*
Zucchini with Parmesan*
Green Salad
Chocolate Mousse*

Jellied Consommé
Chicken Fricassee*
Dumplings*
Broccoli with Mushrooms*
Apple Pie and Cheese

Mussels on the Half Shell*
Chicken Breasts in Foil*
Boston Brown Bread*
Green Peas*
Strawberry Ice Cream

Steamed Clams*
Chicken Stuffed with Onions*
Rice*
Green Beans
Fig Pudding*

Oyster Cocktail
Steam-Roast Stuffed Turkey*
Belgian Endive*
Sweet Potatoes
Plum Pudding*

Stuffed Mushrooms*
Orange Duck*
Whole Wheat Dumplings*
Puréed Spinach*
Berry Pie

Half Grapefruit
Goose in Red Wine*
Short-Cut Biscuit Dumplings*
Currant Jelly
Okra*
Bavarian Cream

Corn in Husks on a Grill*
Baby Pheasant*
Jelly
Celery and Mushrooms*
Cherry Pot Pie*

CHINESE I
Chinese Chicken with Ginger*
Chinese Rice*
Chinese Cabbage with Mushrooms*
Pineapple
Almond Cookies

CHINESE II
Fish Fillets Oriental Style*
Chinese Chicken with Mushrooms*
Rice*
Red-Cooked Chinese Cabbage*
Kumquats   Fortune Cookies

Meat

Mushrooms au Naturel*
Pot Roast with Prunes*
Horseradish Sauce
Mashed Potatoes
Glazed Carrots*
Orange Pudding*

Mussels on the Half Shell*
Pork with Mushrooms*
Cauliflower*
Green Beans
Pears in Red Wine*

Fresh Fruit Cup
White Lamb Stew*
Dumplings*
Baked Tomatoes
Watercress Salad
Sponge Cake*

Mushroom Soup
Veal Paprikash*
Noodles
Broccoli*
Tomato and Green Salad
Almond Pudding*

Chicken Consommé
Osso Bucco*
Rice*
Cauliflower Purée*
Italian Spinach*
Light Orange Pudding*

Asparagus*
Pork Tenderloin in Sauce*
Applesauce*
Zucchini with Parmesan*
Tomato Aspic
Pumpkin Pie

Japanese Shrimp with Mushrooms*
Pork Balls with Rice*
Rolls*
French Peas*
Mixed Salad
Lemon Custard*

Cold Shrimp*
Rack of Lamb*
Glazed Carrots*
Purée of Broccoli
Foil-Baked Bananas*

Green Beans with Shallots*
Pork Loin*
Short-Cut Biscuit Dumplings*
Acorn Squash*
Tomato Salad
Chestnut Chocolate Pudding*

Fish and Shell-fish

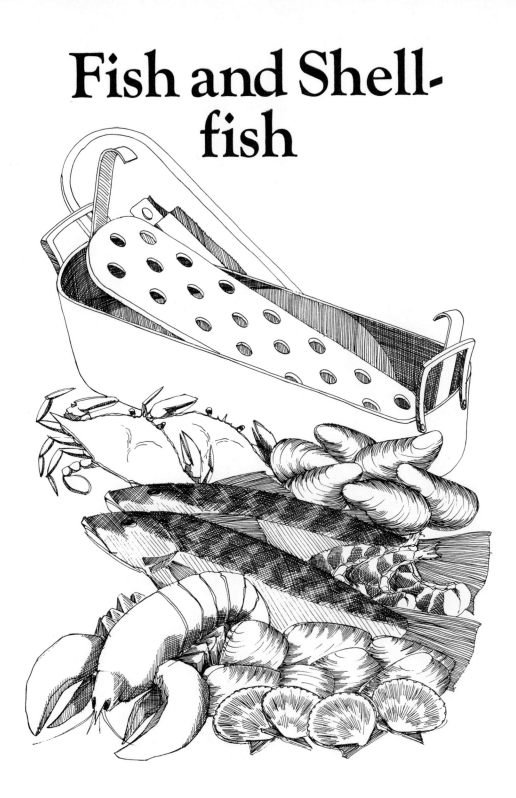

Fish is one of the great foods of the world. It is available all over in great variety. Your doctor recommends it because it is easily digestible, low in calories, high in protein and minerals. But don't let that spoil it for you. The delicate taste of fish is one of the greatest gourmet pleasures.

Fish is easily cooked, and the best of all possible methods of cooking fish is by steaming. Fish steamed in foil loses not a whiff of its delicate flavor. You can vary the flavor to suit your mood by adding good things to the foil package: butter, scallions, dill, tomato, lemon, wine, enriching the delicious aroma that escapes when the package is opened. And it doesn't escape prematurely. Your husband doesn't come home, sniff the air, and say, "Oh, fish for dinner!" It's all saved up until dinnertime. And after dinner, there's no cleanup. It's all in the foil.

And fish in foil is so easy to serve. Fish in individual foil packages can go straight to the table, where they are a conversation piece as each diner opens his own.

A whole large fish is another impressive conversation piece if you can get it out of the pan in one piece. But even with four hands and two spatulas, the creature is almost certain to break. The answer is foil. When done to a delicate turn, you roll the fish out of its wrapping onto a warm platter, or better still serve it from the foil with the edges pushed down on the platter. Serving is even easier if you (or your fishmonger) have removed the center bone before cooking.

Of course you steam shellfish. Clams, mussels *marinière,* crabs, and lobsters all profit by steaming.

A word of warning: Never overcook any seafood. Fish lightly steamed and delicately flavored is the best of good eating.

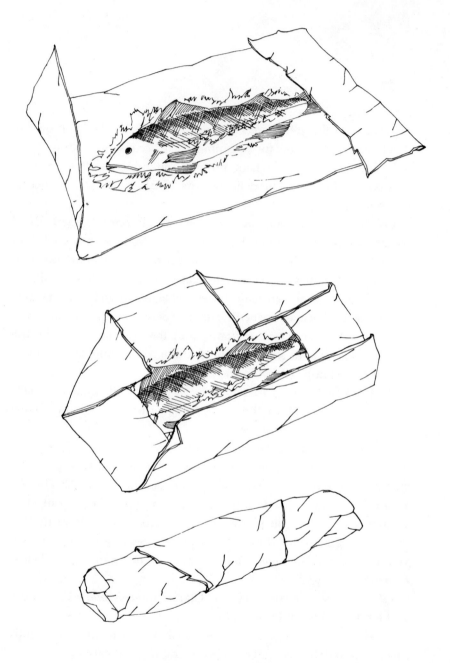

STUFFED BASS

1 3½-pound bass
2 scallions, chopped fine
2 tablespoons butter
1 pound mushrooms, chopped
½ clove garlic, crushed
  (optional)

¾ cup bread crumbs
1 teaspoon salt
¼ teaspoon pepper
Melted butter
Lemon wedges

Leave the head and tail on the fish. Sauté the scallions in butter for a few minutes, add the mushrooms, and cook and stir for about 2 minutes until they give their juice. Add the garlic, bread crumbs, salt, and pepper. Stuff the fish, closing the cavity with toothpicks or poultry pins, or sew it shut. Place on the rack of a steamer or on a piece of foil on the rack. Steam for 20 minutes for small fish, 30 for a 4-pound one. You can steam in a 375° oven, cooking for 10 minutes longer. If using foil, steam 10 minutes longer and serve with juices poured over. If using a rack, serve with a little melted butter and lemon juice poured over if you wish. Serve with lemon wedges.

SERVES 6

BASS STUFFED WITH MUSSELS

3 pounds mussels
¼ cup white wine
¼ cup water
1 cup bread crumbs
3 tablespoons chopped parsley

3 tablespoons melted butter
1 large clove garlic, minced
1 bass, 3½ to 4 pounds
1 teaspoon salt
2 teaspoons lemon juice

Scrub the mussels and debeard. Steam in the wine and water for 3 or 4 minutes until they open. Remove mussels from their shells and strain the liquid, avoiding any sand in the bottom of the pot.

Combine the mussels with crumbs, parsley, butter, and garlic. Add enough mussel liquid to moisten. Wash and dry the fish and place it on a large sheet of heavy foil. Sprinkle it with salt and lemon juice. Stuff the fish and secure the opening. Pour the remaining liquid over. Close the foil, being sure to seal the sides so no juice can escape. Bake at 400° for 45 minutes. Serve in the foil. If you open it at the table, the fragrance will delight everyone. However, you can open it and fold under or cut off the side of the foil. Do not try to lift the fish off the foil; it will break.

SERVES 6 TO 8

CHINESE BASS

1 sea bass, 4 to 4½ pounds
2 tablespoons peanut or
　vegetable oil
1 teaspoon salt
½ teaspoon pepper
1 teaspoon sugar
2 tablespoons mashed black
　beans

2 tablespoons soy sauce
2 tablespoons hoisin, sake, or
　sherry
1-inch piece ginger root,
　shredded
4 scallions, slivered

Leave the head and tail on the fish. Make 3 or 4 diagonal slashes on each side. Rub the fish inside and out with the oil. Combine the salt, pepper, sugar, and beans; spread it on both sides of the fish. Place it in a steamer or on a platter in a pot with a tight-fitting lid. If you have neither, place it on a large sheet of foil. Combine the soy and hoisin (sake or sherry) and pour it on the fish; sprinkle with ginger and scallions. If using a pot, put 3 inches of water in the bottom and steam the fish for 25 minutes. If using foil, fold it envelope fashion so no juice can escape. Bake it in a preheated 350° oven for 45 minutes.

SERVES 6 TO 8

FLOUNDER WITH LEMON AND ORANGE

1 3½-pound flounder
1 tablespoon lemon juice
1 tablespoon orange juice
  concentrate or 3 tablespoons
  juice

1 teaspoon salt
¼ teaspoon pepper
½ teaspoon paprika

Wipe and dry the fish, leaving the head and tail on. Combine the remaining ingredients. Place the fish on a large piece of buttered or oiled foil. Cover with the mixed fruit juice and seasonings. Wrap securely in the foil and bake at 400° for about 30 minutes. You may cook the fish on the rack of a steamer if you wish.

SERVES 6

HERBED BLUEFISH

1 bluefish, 3 to 4 pounds
1 teaspoon salt
¼ teaspoon pepper
1 tablespoon minced fresh or 2
  teaspoons dried dill

3 tablespoons minced parsley
2 tablespoons minced chives
2 teaspoons lemon juice
Grated rind ½ lemon

Wash and dry the fish. Leave the head and tail on. Rub inside and out with the salt and pepper combined with the herbs. Pour on the lemon juice and rind. Fold the foil over, securing the ends tight. Bake at 400° for 40 minutes. If you want the fish brown, raise heat to 450° and open the foil for the last 15 minutes of cooking.

SERVES 6 TO 8

POMPANO

1 pompano, about 2 pounds   4 scallions
2 tablespoons soft butter   2 tablespoons sherry
1 teaspoon salt

Put the pompano on a heatproof platter or piece of foil on the rack of a steamer. Spread with butter and sprinkle with salt and scallions. Add the sherry and steam for about 25 minutes.

SERVES 4

RED SNAPPER STUFFED WITH CLAMS

1 red snapper, 4 to 5 pounds   2 tablespoons butter
½ teaspoon salt   1 cup bread crumbs
¼ teaspoon pepper   1 7-ounce can minced clams
3 scallions, chopped   1 egg, beaten

Wash the fish and rub the outside with salt and pepper. Place on a large sheet of buttered foil. Sauté the scallions in butter and stir in the bread crumbs. Remove from heat and add the clams and their juice. Add the egg, beaten with a tablespoon or two of water. Fill the fish and fasten the opening with poultry pins or toothpicks. Close the foil, folding it carefully so no juice can escape. Cook on a steamer rack for 50 minutes or bake in a 375° oven for 45 minutes. If you want the top browned, open the foil and cook in the oven for the last 10 minutes of the cooking time at 450°. Lift the fish onto a platter in its foil. Other fish such as bass, lake trout, mackerel, or haddock may be cooked this same way.

SERVES 6 TO 8

SALMON IN ASPIC

1 4½-pound piece or 1
   5-pound whole salmon
1 teaspoon salt
½ teaspoon pepper
Few sprigs fresh or 1 teaspoon
   dried dill
Few sprigs fresh or ½ teaspoon
   dry thyme
2 sprigs parsley
2 bay leaves
Few celery leaves
3 cups water
1 envelope gelatin

½ cup white wine or dry
   vermouth
1 egg white, beaten
GARNISHES: sprigs of dill,
   parsley, or tarragon; sliced
   stuffed green olives or black
   olives, carrots or pimiento,
   thin slices lemon
SAUCE (optional):
   mayonnaise, green
   mayonnaise, Louis, and/or
   lemon wedges

Place the salmon on a piece of foil or a double thickness of cheesecloth on the rack of a steamer. Fold the foil or cheesecloth over loosely. Combine the salt, pepper, dill, thyme, parsley, bay leaves, and celery leaves with the water and put into the lower part of the steamer. Steam for 40 minutes, turn off the heat, and let the fish rest with the lid on the steamer for 20 minutes. Lift out and pull and scrape the skin off. It is easy while the fish is still warm. Roll out on a cold platter and remove skin from the other side. Boil the liquid down to a little more than a cup. Strain. Soften the gelatin in the hot liquid and add the white wine and egg white. Heat gently while stirring. Cool until syrupy and spoon a thin layer over the fish. Chill the fish until the aspic is set. Decorate with some of the suggested garnishes or use any you wish. Cover with remaining aspic. If the aspic has gotten too firm, warm it slightly. Chill until set. Serve the salmon with a sauce and/or lemon wedges.

SERVES 8 TO 10

SALMON, HOT OR COLD

1 3½-pound piece of salmon
1 teaspoon lemon juice
1 bay leaf, crushed
Few celery leaves

Few sprigs parsley
½ cup white wine or dry
   vermouth
Lemon wedges

Place the salmon on a piece of foil, sprinkle with lemon juice, and surround with remaining ingredients except lemon wedges. Fold and pinch the foil closed. Steam in a 375° oven for 45 minutes. If you are going to serve the salmon cold, cool slightly in the foil and then remove any skin or bones. Chill again before serving. If serving hot, spoon some of the liquid over the fish on a warm platter. Serve either with wedges of lemon.

SERVES 8

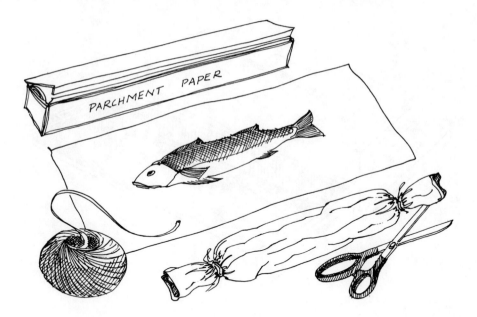

TROUT IN PAPER
(En Papillote)

---

*1 sea or lake trout, 4½ to 5½
   pounds*
1 teaspoon salt
½ teaspoon pepper

*2 teaspoons lemon juice
   (optional)*
3 tablespoons soft butter

Leave the head and tail on the trout. Sprinkle with salt and
pepper, and lemon juice if you wish. Cut waxed paper, parchment,
or brown paper large enough to wrap around the fish and butter
the parchment or brown paper. Place the fish on the buttered side
and roll the paper around the fish. Tie the ends tight with string.
Put in a shallow baking pan and bake at 400° for 40 minutes.
Remove to a warm platter, cut the string, and unwrap at the table.

SERVES 8

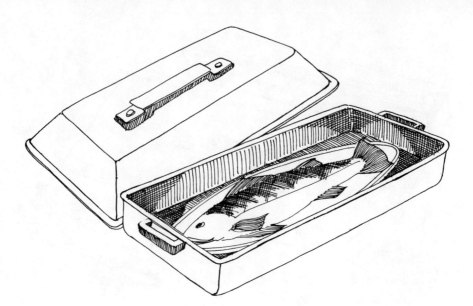

WHITEFISH *

1 whitefish, 3½ to 4 pounds
½ pound ham, slivered or
 diced
¼ pound bacon, salt pork, or
 ham fat, sliced

½ cup sherry
1 teaspoon salt
Lemon wedges

Have the head and tail left on the fish but have the center bone removed if possible. This facilitates serving, but is not essential. Score both sides of the fish and place it on a greased platter that will fit inside a steamer. A roasting pan is good for this if the top fits tight. Combine the ham with bacon (salt pork or ham fat), sherry, and salt and spoon it over and inside the fish. Put water in the bottom of the steamer or pan, being sure it does not come up to the edge of the platter. You may have to prop up the platter if using a roaster. Steam for 25 minutes. Serve on the platter it was steamed in, with lemon wedges.

SERVES 6 TO 8

* Any white-flesh fish may be substituted, such as lake trout.

LARGE FISH IN FOIL

---

1 fish, 3½ to 4 pounds: bass,
  lake trout, scrod, bluefish,
  pompano, or snapper
2 teaspoons salt
½ teaspoon pepper
Few lettuce leaves

2 tablespoons butter
2 or 3 scallions, slivered
  (optional)
Melted butter and lemon
  wedges

Leave the head and tail on the fish. Place on a sheet of foil large enough to wrap the fish. Sprinkle inside and out with salt and pepper. Add a few lettuce leaves, butter, and, if you wish, the scallions. Wrap the fish envelope fashion so no juice can escape. Place in a 350° oven and bake for about 45 minutes. You can easily roll the fish onto a warm platter, juices and all, or place the foil on a platter to serve. Pass melted butter and lemon wedges.

SERVES 6 TO 8

Variations

HERBED FISH IN FOIL

Add a pinch of thyme, 2 tablespoons minced fresh dill, dried oregano, or rosemary, and 2 tablespoons minced parsley to Fish in Foil.*

FISH IN FOIL WITH ONION

Add 3 scallions, slivered, or 1 small onion, sliced thin, to Herbed Fish in Foil.*

HAWAIIAN FISH IN TI LEAVES

1 3½-pound piece of fish: cod,
  scrod, bass, red snapper,
  trout, or halibut
1 teaspoon salt

½ teaspoon pepper
⅛ pound salt pork
1 lemon, sliced
Ti leaves or foil

Rub fish with salt and pepper and dot with pieces of salt pork. Add the lemon. Wrap in ti leaves if you can get them; tie with string. You may wrap in foil folded envelope fashion. Bake at 350° for about 45 minutes.

SERVES 6

FISH WITH BLACK BEANS

1 3½-pound fish: sea or black
  bass, lake or sea trout
4 scallions, chopped
½ cup soy sauce
1 clove garlic, crushed

1 tablespoon black beans
  (fermented, if available)
2 tablespoons oil
2 teaspoons lemon juice

Clean the fish, leaving head and tail on. Combine half the scallions, half the soy sauce, garlic, and the black beans. Place the fish on a platter in a steamer or on a piece of foil. Spread with the bean mixture inside and out. Cover the steamer or fold the foil closed and steam on a rack for 35 minutes, or bake 40 minutes in foil in a 400° oven. Sauté the remaining scallions in oil, add the remaining soy sauce and the lemon juice and pour over the fish.

SERVES 6

FISH WITH BEAN CURD
(Tofu)

---

1 3½-pound fish or 2½ pounds
    slices
1 tablespoon agi-no-moto or
    monosodium glutamate
2 pieces soy bean curd
3 eggs
1 scallion, minced

2 small carrots, minced
¼ cup green peas
1 teaspoon salt
2 teaspoons sugar
1 tablespoon soy sauce
Lemon slices

Sprinkle the fish with agi-no-moto or monosodium glutamate. Squeeze the bean curd in a piece of cloth to remove moisture and crumble it. Beat the eggs slightly. Add the remaining ingredients except lemon slices and stir well. Spread the mixture over the fish. If using a whole fish put on both sides and in cavity; use pins or toothpicks to close fish. Place a cloth or piece of foil on the rack of a steamer and fold lightly over the fish. Steam for 25 minutes for whole fish, 12 for small pieces. Lift out onto warm platter or plates. It is easy to lift it on cloth or foil without breaking the fish. You may steam this, tightly wrapped in foil, in a 400° oven. It will take 30 to 35 minutes. Serve with lemon slices on top.

SERVES 6

SWEET AND SOUR FISH

1 fish, 3½ to 4 pounds: mullet,
  carp, or bass
10 ounces crushed pineapple
  with juice

2 tablespoons sugar
2 tablespoons vinegar
1 teaspoon salt
2 teaspoons soy sauce

Clean the fish, leaving the head and tail on. Place it on a sheet of foil. Combine the remaining ingredients and spoon the mixture inside, around, and over the fish. Close the foil and bake for 40 minutes at 350° or steam it in a steamer for 40 minutes. Serve with all the juices poured over.

SERVES 6 TO 8

FISH WITH SOY AND GINGER

1 white-flesh fish, such as trout,
  bass, bluefish, or scrod, 3½
  to 4 pounds
½ teaspoon salt
½ cup coarsely chopped
  scallions

½ cup coarsely chopped parsley
¼ cup soy sauce
¼ cup chopped fresh ginger
  root

Clean the fish, leaving head and tail on, and sprinkle with salt. Place on a piece of cheesecloth or foil on the rack of a steamer. Combine the remaining ingredients and put about half inside the fish and the remainder over the top. Steam for 35 minutes if on cloth, 45 minutes if on foil. Remove carefully to a warm platter and, if you've used foil, pour any juices over.

SERVES 6

FISH IN SEAWEED

(You must have fresh seaweed for this recipe. Sometimes the fish market can supply it if you are not by the sea.)

1 3½-pound sea trout, bass, or snapper	*¼ teaspoon pepper*
1 teaspoon salt	*Fresh seaweed*
	½ cup water

Rub the fish inside with salt and pepper. Place it on half the seaweed in a casserole. Put the remaining seaweed on top. Add the water, cover tight, and steam for 25 minutes. To serve, remove the top seaweed and serve the fish in its nest in the casserole. To carve, remove the fish to a heated platter.

SERVES 6

FISH WITH WHITE WINE SAUCE

1 2½-pound whitefish or trout   1½ cups milk
3 tablespoons butter   1 teaspoon salt
3 tablespoons flour   ¼ teaspoon pepper
2 tablespoons Worcestershire   ¼ cup dry white wine
    sauce

Wrap the fish in cheesecloth and place on a rack over a few inches of boiling water. Cover the pot tight and steam for 20 minutes. Meanwhile, make the sauce by melting the butter, blending in the flour—do not brown. Stir in the Worcestershire sauce and milk slowly; add salt and pepper. Cook and stir until thickened. Add the wine and turn off the heat. Serve the fish on a warm platter with sauce poured over.

SERVES 4

FISH ON A GRILL

1 4-pound fish or a 3½-pound   ¼ teaspoon pepper
    piece of fish   Soft butter or oil
1 teaspoon salt   2 tablespoons lemon juice

If using a whole fish, leave the head and tail on. If using a center cut, leave the bone in. Sprinkle the fish with salt and pepper. Brush a large piece of heavy foil with butter or oil. Place the fish on the foil and pour the lemon juice over. Fold the foil over envelope fashion so no juice can escape. Place over a grill about 5 inches above the not-too-hot coals and cook for 45 minutes. Serve in the foil or roll out onto a warm platter, pouring all juices over.

SERVES 6 TO 8

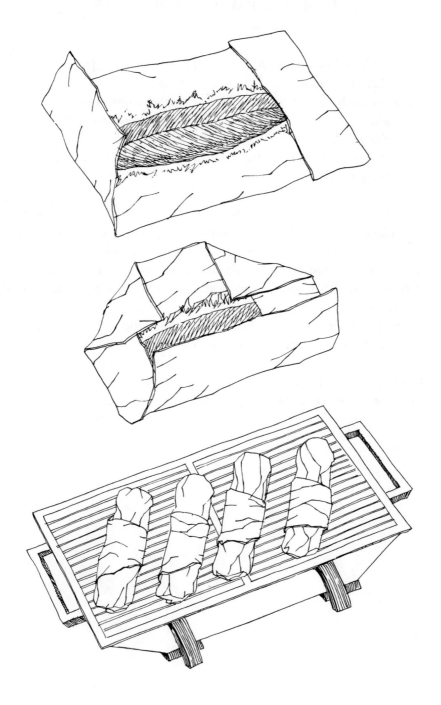

FISH WITH EGG SAUCE

1 fish, 3½ to 4 pounds, or 3
  pounds pieces of fish
1 teaspoon salt
EGG SAUCE:
  2 tablespoons flour
  2 tablespoons butter, melted
  ½ teaspoon salt

1 cup fish broth (from
  steamed fish)
1 teaspoon lemon juice
2 tablespoons hard butter, cut
  into pieces
2 hard-cooked eggs, chopped

Use any not-too-oily white-flesh fish. Sprinkle the fish with salt and place on the rack of a steamer on a piece of cheesecloth or other cloth. Put very little water in the bottom of the steamer, about 2 inches. Steam for 30 minutes. Remove to a heated platter; it's easy if the fish is wrapped in cloth. Start the sauce while the fish is steaming.

Stir the flour into the melted butter and add the salt. When smooth, slowly pour in a cup of the water from the steamer while stirring steadily. Simmer and stir for several minutes. Add the lemon juice, the hard butter in pieces, and then the chopped eggs. Pour the sauce over the fish or pass in a separate dish.

SERVES 6 TO 8

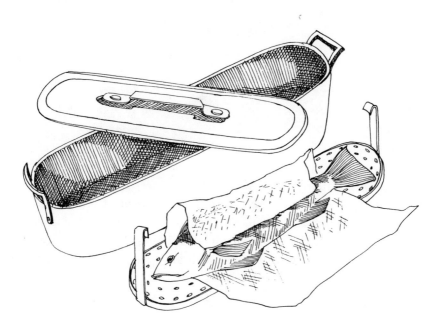

FISH IN CHEESECLOTH

1 3½-pound fish or 2½ pounds
   fish fillets
1 teaspoon salt
1 clove garlic or 1 small onion,
   minced

2 tablespoons minced celery
¼ cup white vinegar
2 tablespoons chopped parsley
Melted butter (optional)
Lemon wedges (optional)

Place the fish on a piece of cheesecloth large enough to cover it. Place in a steamer or on a rack a few inches above the surface of the water in a large pot. Have about 2 inches of water in the bottom of the utensil. Sprinkle the fish with salt, garlic or onion, and the celery. Put the vinegar into the water. Steam for about 25 minutes for a whole fish, 20 for fillets. Remove to a warm platter by lifting the fish up gently in the cheesecloth and rolling it onto the platter. Sprinkle with parsley and serve with melted butter and lemon wedges if you wish.

SERVES 6

HALIBUT

---

1 2½-pound piece of halibut
2 tablespoons white wine
2 tablespoons olive oil
1 teaspoon salt

¼ teaspoon pepper
1 tablespoon soy sauce or 1
    teaspoon lemon juice
2 scallions, slivered

Remove any bones from the halibut if you can do so without breaking up the piece of fish. Place the halibut on a piece of foil. Add the remaining ingredients. Fold the foil shut, envelope fashion. Bake in a preheated 350° oven for 40 minutes. Serve on a warm platter, rolling the fish off the foil with any juices. Or serve in the foil, if you wish.

SERVES 6

BROOK TROUT

---

6 trout, ¾ pound each
3 tablespoons melted butter
1 teaspoon lemon juice

1 teaspoon salt
Lemon wedges

Clean the trout, leaving heads and tails on. Place each on a square of foil large enough to cover the fish. Brush with butter mixed with lemon juice. Sprinkle with salt. Fold the foil over envelope fashion so no juice can escape. Steam in a 400° oven for 25 minutes. You may roll out on a warm platter or plate or serve in the foil and let each open his own aromatic trout. Serve with lemon wedges.

SERVES 6

SMALL FISH WITH SHERRY

---

4 small perch or trout or 8 large
   smelt
¼ cup sherry

2 shallots, minced
4 teaspoons olive oil or butter
1 teaspoon salt

Clean the fish, leaving the heads and tails on. Make diagonal slashes on both sides. Put the fish on a plate in a little sherry and pour the remaining sherry over. Let marinate at least 30 minutes. Put fish on another plate, pour the sherry over, and put remaining ingredients on the fish. Steam for 20 minutes. If steaming in foil in the oven, cook at 400° for 30 minutes.

SERVES 4

SMELTS

---

3 pounds smelts
1½ teaspoons salt
¼ teaspoon pepper
1 tablespoon dill

2 tablespoons minced parsley
2 tablespoons grated onion
   (optional)
2 tablespoons butter

Have the fish cleaned, leaving heads and tails on. Place on a large sheet of foil or use six small sheets. Sprinkle with salt, pepper, dill, and parsley, and the onion if you wish. Divide the butter among the fish. Wrap securely in the foil and bake at 400° for about 20 minutes. You may open the foil for the last 5 minutes of cooking and raise the heat to 450° to brown the fish if you wish.

SERVES 6

SHAD

---

2 skinned, boned fillets of shad
  (1 fish)
1 scallion, slivered
1 teaspoon salt

2 tablespoons sherry, white
  wine, or vermouth
Lemon wedges

Place the fillets on a sheet of foil, sprinkle with scallions and salt. Add the wine and close the foil tight, pinching it at the top to prevent any liquid from leaking. Steam for 30 minutes in a 375° oven. If you want the fish browned, open the foil after 20 minutes, turn the oven up to 425°, and brown for 10 minutes. Serve with lemon wedges.

SERVES 4 TO 6

FILLETS OF FLOUNDER

---

6 fillets of flounder (not more
  than ½ pound each)
Soft butter
½ teaspoon dried basil
1 teaspoon salt

¼ teaspoon pepper
¼ cup slivered scallions
2 tomatoes, peeled and chopped
1 tablespoon wine or wine
  vinegar

Place the fillets on 6 sheets of lightly buttered foil and sprinkle with basil, salt, and pepper. Divide the scallions and tomatoes among the packages, adding the wine or vinegar. Fold the foil, pinching it shut securely. Bake at 400° for 35 minutes. Serve in the foil packages to retain all juices and fragrance.

SERVES 6

FILLET OF FLOUNDER WITH TOMATOES

2½ pounds fillets of flounder
1 teaspoon salt
¼ teaspoon pepper
½ teaspoon sugar
¼ teaspoon thyme

1½ cups canned or fresh
  tomatoes, chopped
1 tablespoon minced onion or
  ¼ teaspoon minced garlic
2 tablespoons olive oil or butter

Place the fillets on a large piece of foil or divide the fish among 6 small pieces of foil. Add a mixture of the remaining ingredients. If using fresh tomatoes, peel them before chopping. Close the foil, folding carefully so no juice can escape. Place in a preheated 400° oven and cook for about 30 minutes, about 5 minutes less for single packages. Good served in the foil but these will turn out easily onto a warm platter.

SERVES 6

FISH FILLETS WITH HAM

---

6 fish fillets (about ⅓ pound
  each)
6 thin slices of ham
2 tablespoons butter

½ teaspoon salt
¼ teaspoon pepper
1 tablespoon lemon juice or
  vermouth

Place the fillets on the ham, cut about the size of the fillets. Place on squares of foil or on one large piece or on a piece of parchment. Dot with butter and sprinkle with salt, pepper, and either lemon juice or vermouth. Fold the foil over, sealing the edges tight. Bake in a preheated 425° oven for 25 minutes.

SERVES 6

FISH FILLETS ON A GRILL

2½ *pounds fish fillets such as*
  flounder, sole, trout, or cod
Few shreds lettuce

1 tablespoon minced parsley
2 scallions, slivered
6 teaspoons butter

Cut the fish into 18 strips and roll each up. Secure with tooth-picks until ready to use. You may remove the toothpicks as you place the rolls on foil. If you leave the toothpicks in, be sure they do not pierce the foil. Place on a sheet of buttered foil or use 6 small pieces if you wish. Add the remaining ingredients. Fold tight and place over coals. Steam for about 25 minutes.

SERVES 6

FISH FILLETS ORIENTAL STYLE

2½ *pounds fish fillets: sole,*
  flounder, or other white fish
3 ounces dried mushrooms
3 scallions, shredded
1½ *tablespoons shredded*
  ginger root or 1 teaspoon
  powdered

½ *teaspoon salt*
½ *teaspoon pepper*
2 tablespoons soy sauce
2 tablespoons peanut oil

Rinse the fish in cold water and cut it into serving-size pieces. Place on a platter or plate. Choose one that will fit into a pot or steamer. Meanwhile, soak the mushrooms for 30 minutes in water, drain and cut into slivers, removing tough stems. Combine with the remaining ingredients and spread over the fish. Cover the pot tight and steam for about 10 minutes.

SERVES 6

HAWAIIAN FISH AND SPINACH

1 pound spinach
2½ pounds sole or flounder
  fillets
1 teaspoon salt or 1 tablespoon
  soy sauce

½ teaspoon pepper
1 cup coconut milk

Wash the spinach thoroughly and cut away any heavy tough stems. Divide among four pieces of greased foil. Top with the fish fillets. Sprinkle the salt or soy sauce and pepper over. Add the coconut milk. Fold the foil and seal tight. In Hawaii ti leaves are used in place of foil. Steam on the rack of a steamer or bake at 400° for about 35 minutes.

SERVES 6

SALMON STEAK

4 salmon steaks (about 6 ounces
  each)
1 teaspoon salt
¼ teaspoon pepper
1 tablespoon lemon juice

1 teaspoon minced onion
  (optional)
3 tablespoons clam juice or fish
  broth
Lemon wedges

Place each piece of salmon on a square of foil. Sprinkle with salt, pepper, lemon juice, and the onion if you wish. Pour the clam juice or fish broth over. Seal the foil tight and cook for 30 minutes in a preheated 375° oven. Serve in the foil if you wish or turn out on heated plates or a platter. Pass lemon wedges.

SERVES 4

COD STEAKS WITH GINGER

2 to 2½ pounds cod steaks
1 teaspoon salt or 2 teaspoons
  soy sauce
2 teaspoons chopped ginger

1 scallion, minced
1 tablespoon minced parsley
1 tablespoon vermouth or white
  wine

Place the cod on a heatproof dish that will fit into a steamer or pot. Add the remaining ingredients, cover with a piece of foil, and steam in a 400° oven for about 25 minutes. Serve in the dish. You may cook the cod the same way in foil in the oven, buttering the foil lightly.

SERVES 4 TO 6

PORTUGUESE SALT COD

1 1½-pound piece salt cod
4 potatoes, peeled and sliced
4 onions, peeled and sliced
3 tomatoes, peeled and sliced
1 piece pimiento, sliced thin

2 tablespoons olive oil
2 tablespoons white wine
½ teaspoon salt
¼ teaspoon pepper

Soak the cod for at least 12 hours, changing the water twice. Flake the fish. Combine the remaining ingredients. Layer into a casserole or heatproof bowl, starting with the vegetables, then a layer of cod, vegetables, cod, and vegetables. Pour the oil and wine over and add seasonings. Cover tight. If you do not have a lid for the utensil, cover with a double layer of foil held tight with a rubber band. Put into a 375° oven or on a rack of a steamer and cook for 1½ hours.

SERVES 4

ORIENTAL FISH AND PASTA

¾ *pound vermicelli, cooked*
2 egg whites, slightly whipped
2 tablespoons soy or shoyu sauce

1½ pounds fish fillets in 6
pieces
¼ *cup fish broth or clam juice*

Cook the vermicelli 5 minutes only and rinse in a strainer. Toss with the egg whites mixed with 1 tablespoon soy or shoyu sauce. Place the fish fillets in 6 small deep bowls or a large bowl or on a platter. Arrange the vermicelli around the fish. Combine the remaining soy sauce with fish broth or clam juice and pour over the fish and vermicelli. Steam for 10 minutes, no longer.

SERVES 6

JAPANESE FISH AND MUSHROOMS

1 pound mushrooms
2 pounds white-flesh fish, cut up
¼ *cup sake or sherry*
1 tablespoon shoyu sauce

½ *bunch watercress*
½ *cup fish broth, dashi, or*
chicken broth
Juice of 1 lemon

Cut the mushrooms into pieces and combine with the fish. Pour the sake (or sherry) and shoyu sauce over and let stand for half an hour. Remove tough stems from the watercress and break into pieces about 1½ inches long. Add to the fish and put into six small bowls or 1 large bowl on a steamer. Add the fish broth (dashi or chicken broth) and lemon juice. Steam for 20 minutes.

SERVES 6

Japanese steamed food, *Mushi,* is often cooked in bowls and the food served in the same bowl.

JAPANESE FISH WITH SHOYU AND SALT

2½ pounds cod, sea bass, or
 other white-flesh fish
1 teaspoon salt
¼ cup shoyu sauce
1 tablespoon rice wine vinegar

1 tablespoon lemon juice
2 Japanese or other white
 radishes, grated
1 teaspoon sugar

Cut the fish in slices and rub on all sides with salt. Place on a plate or in a bowl and sprinkle with 1 tablespoon shoyu sauce. Steam for 20 minutes. Meanwhile, make a sauce by combining the remaining shoyu with vinegar, lemon juice, grated radish, and sugar. Serve the sauce as a dip.

SERVES 6

FISH AND EGG CUSTARD

1 pound cod or any white fish,
  ground
½ pound shrimp, ground
1 (7-ounce) can minced clams,
  ground

8 eggs
2 cups water
1½ teaspoons salt
2 teaspoons soy sauce

Combine the fish, shrimp, and clams, saving any liquid. Beat the eggs with clam liquid, water, salt, and soy sauce. Add the fish to the eggs and blend together. Pour into a baking dish. Place on the rack of a steamer or in a deep pot with a tight-fitting lid. Steam for 15 to 20 minutes.

SERVES 8

FISH MOLD

1½ pounds cod, haddock, or
  any white-flesh fish
½ cup butter
⅓ cup flour
4 eggs, separated

1 cup cream
1 teaspoon salt
¼ teaspoon pepper
1 teaspoon dried dill
Parsley for garnish (optional)

Remove any skin and bones from the fish and put into a blender or food processor with the butter. Blend until smooth. Stir the flour into the slightly beaten egg yolks. Add the cream slowly. Season with salt, pepper, and dill. Combine this gradually with the fish, stirring steadily. Fold in the stiffly beaten egg whites. Pour into a buttered and floured mold or bowl. Cover and steam for an hour. Unmold onto a warm platter. Garnish with parsley if you wish.

SERVES 4

Shellfish, fortunately, is available fresh or frozen all over the United States. It is most important that fresh shellfish is *fresh*. One way to be sure is if it's alive! Lobsters must be alive unless they have been cooked before you buy them; shells of oysters, clams, and mussels must be closed tight; shrimp should be a greenish gray color (there are a few varieties that are pink) and they should fit tight in their shells.

Shellfish is delicious and, like other fish, should not be overcooked.

STEAMED CLAMS

6 pounds (about 8 dozen) soft clams
1 tablespoon lemon juice
Melted butter

Scrub the clams under running water. There are several possible ways to have clams eliminate their sand. Soaking in salted cold water, 1 tablespoon salt to 1 quart of water, for several hours, or a cup of corn meal added to the water, may help. Rinse the clams thoroughly if you have used the corn meal. Put the clams in a large pot with about 1½ inches of water in the bottom. You may put them in the rack of a steamer with no more than 1½ inches of water in the bottom. Cover tight and steam until the clams open, about 10 to 12 minutes. Add lemon juice to the melted butter and serve very hot in small individual dishes. Or serve the clams from a warm soup tureen or in soup plates. Pour the liquid into cups or glasses. Avoid any sand deposit in the bottom of the steamer. To eat, dip each clam, held by the neck, into the broth and then into the butter. The clam broth is delicious to drink.

SERVES 4

STEAMED CLAMS WITH TOMATOES

6 pounds soft clams
2 tablespoons oil, preferably
  olive
2 cloves garlic, minced

4 large tomatoes, peeled, or 1
  (10-ounce) can Italian plum
  tomatoes
Salt

Steam the clams as for Steamed Clams* and when cool enough to handle remove from their shells. Boil the broth down to half its strength and strain through a fine sieve or piece of cheesecloth. Put the oil into a saucepan, add garlic and then tomatoes, the clam broth, and salt to taste. The amount depends on how salty the clams are—go slow. Bring to a boil, add the clams, and cook only to heat them through.

SERVES 4

CLAMS À LA MARINARA

6 dozen littleneck clams
2 cloves garlic, minced
1 medium onion, minced
2 tablespoons olive oil
2 tablespoons finely chopped
  parsley

1 tomato, peeled and chopped,
  or 2 tablespoons tomato paste
¼ cup white wine
Salt

Soak the clams for an hour. Scrub them and wash them under running water. Put the garlic and onion in a pot with the oil. Heat for a few minutes. Add the clams, parsley, tomato, and wine. Steam until the clams open, about 8 minutes. Add salt to taste.

SERVES 6

CLAMBAKE

2 2½-pound chickens,   8 small lobster tails or 4
   quartered   1-pound lobsters, split
12 to 16 new potatoes, scrubbed   8 to 10 ears of corn, with corn
32 clams, scrubbed   silk pulled out

If you have a clam steamer, use it; if not, use a big pot with a tight-fitting lid. If using a pot, fit a rack or piece of metal up several inches from the bottom. Balance it on some clean rocks or a bowl. The water, 3 or 4 inches of it, goes under this division. Add ¼ cup salt to the water or use sea water. If seaweed is available, put it in the bottom. If not, use any greens such as spinach or chard, about 2 pounds. Layer the other food, except the corn. The lobster, if split, should go on top. Steam about 20 minutes. Add the corn, after dipping it in water, and steam 20 minutes more.

SERVES 8

STEAMED MUSSELS

1 pound mussels per person for first-course serving
1½ to 2 pounds mussels per person for meal serving

Scrub the mussels with a stiff brush under running cold water. Cut the "beard" off with scissors or pull out. You may have to scrape off rough patches on the shells. Let stand in cold water for an hour or two to rid them of sand. To steam, place the mussels in a large pot with a tight-fitting lid. Put about an inch or two of water or white wine or a combination of the two in the pot and steam until the mussels open, about 3 to 5 minutes. The amount of water depends upon the number of mussels used. To serve on the half shell, pull the top shell off and, with a knife, loosen the mussels from the bottom shells. Place the mussels on flat dinner-size plates. Serve with oyster or other small forks.

MUSSELS MARINIÈRE

5 to 6 pounds mussels (4 dozen
if large)
½ cup white wine
3 shallots or 4 scallions, minced
1 large clove garlic, minced or
crushed (optional)

1 bay leaf
1 teaspoon dried thyme
2 tablespoons butter
3 tablespoons minced parsley

Scrub the mussels under running water, scrape if necessary. Strip off the beards with scissors. Place in a deep pot with a tight-fitting lid, add the remaining ingredients, except 2 tablespoons parsley, and steam until the mussels open, about 5 minutes. Serve, sprinkled with remaining parsley, in a soup tureen or in soup plates.

SERVES 4

MUSSELS ON THE HALF SHELL

5 dozen good-size mussels, about 8 pounds
½ cup white wine
2 cloves garlic, minced

1 tablespoon olive oil
¼ cup chopped scallions
2 tablespoons chopped parsley
Lemon wedges (optional)

Scrub and debeard the mussels and steam in white wine until they open, about 5 minutes. Remove and set aside. Put the remaining ingredients with the liquid the mussels were steamed in in a blender. When smooth, taste for salt; you may need a little. Tear the mussels open, discarding the top shells. Loosen each mussel from its shell with the tip of a small knife, leaving the mussels on their shells. Place 6 or 8 on each of 8 plates, with the tips toward the center of the plate. Spoon a little of the sauce over each and let stand for about an hour. Put a lemon wedge in the center of each plate if you wish.

SERVES 8

MUSSELS WITH TOMATO SAUCE

About 4 dozen large steamed mussels, about 6 pounds
2 cups canned tomatoes
2 cloves garlic, chopped

2 tablespoons olive oil
1 teaspoon sugar
1 teaspoon salt

Prepare the mussels as for Steamed Mussels.* When they are cool enough to handle, remove one shell from each and place on a plate. Cool if they are to be served cold. Put the tomatoes, garlic, oil, sugar, and salt in a blender or food processor. Blend for a minute or two. Spoon the sauce over the mussels.

SERVES 4

MUSSELS POULETTE

6 dozen large mussels, about 9
   pounds
½ cup water (or part white
   wine)
3 tablespoons butter

4 tablespoons flour
⅓ cup cream or half-and-half
2 egg yolks, beaten
½ teaspoon lemon juice

Scrub and debeard the mussels and let stand half an hour in cold water. Steam the mussels with the water until they open, about 5 minutes. Make the sauce by melting the butter, stirring in the flour, and adding 1 cup of the liquid the mussels were steamed in. Stir in the cream. Stir and cook until smooth and thickened. Remove from heat and stir in the egg yolks. It is customary to open the mussels, remove one shell, and spoon the sauce over. If you prefer, you may remove the mussels, warm them in the sauce, and serve on rice or toast.

SERVES 6

OYSTERS

36 oysters
½ cup water
1 teaspoon lemon juice
3 tablespoons melted butter

Few drops Tabasco sauce
2 teaspoons Worcestershire
   sauce

Place the oysters in a heavy pot with the water and lemon juice. Cover tight and steam until the oysters begin to open, about 15 minutes. Pull off the top shells. Reduce the liquid to about ¾ cup. Add the butter, Tabasco, and Worcestershire sauce. Taste for seasoning and reheat. Serve on the half shells with hot sauce spooned over.

SERVES 6

STEAMED OYSTERS

24 oysters, scrubbed and rinsed   Melted butter
Salt   Lemon wedges
Pepper

When the oysters are clean, place them on the rack of a steamer and cook until the shells open, about 15 minutes after the water in the steamer comes to a boil. Divide the oysters among four plates after removing the upper shell. Sprinkle with a little salt and pepper. Serve with melted butter and lemon wedges. It is best to have a small cup of melted butter on each oyster plate so each person can dip his oysters in the butter.

SERVES 4

OYSTERS ON A GRILL

48 oysters (large if available)   Crisp bacon (optional)
Melted butter   Lemon wedges

Scrub and rinse the oysters and place on a grill 3 or 4 inches from not-too-hot coals. Steam for about 12 minutes or until shells start to open. Remove with a pancake turner or slotted spoon; they will be hot! Remove top shell. Put 6 oysters on their half shells for each person on a flat plate. Serve hot with a little melted butter or crumbled bacon or both and a lemon wedge.

SERVES 8

SHRIMP — HOT OR COLD

2 pounds medium to large shrimp

Wash the shrimp in several waters. Do not shake them dry. Place in a heavy pot and cook in only the water that clings to the shrimp. Cover and steam for 3 to 4 minutes. Remove shrimp at once or they will be overcooked. Chill or cool and peel or let each peel his own. Serve with lemon wedges, cocktail or other sauce. If to be served hot, you almost have to peel them before serving since they are hard to peel at the table when really hot. In that case, steam no more than 3 minutes. Peel and reheat *very* briefly with a little melted butter and lemon juice. Peeling them before cooking is also acceptable for hot shrimp. Cook them no more than 3 minutes. They will be less moist and a little less tasty than those cooked in their shells.

SERVES 6

SHRIMP IN WINE

1 pound raw shrimp
3 tablespoons white wine, vermouth, or dry sherry
½ teaspoon salt

Peel the shrimp and devein. Place in a dish. Pour the wine over, add the salt, and steam until the shrimp turn pink, about 10 minutes.

SERVES 4

CHINESE SHRIMP

1 pound raw shrimp
2 tablespoons fresh ginger,
   coarsely chopped
1 tablespoon rice wine

1 tablespoon soy sauce
½ cup water chestnuts, sliced
   or diced

Peel and devein the shrimp. Place in a bowl with the remaining ingredients and toss thoroughly. Steam until the shrimp turn pink, about 10 minutes.

SERVES 4

JAPANESE SHRIMP AND MUSHROOMS

½ pound mushrooms
24 medium shrimp, peeled,
   about 1 pound
1 tablespoon soy sauce

2 teaspoons lemon juice
½ teaspoon agi-no-moto or
   monosodium glutamate
2 tablespoons broth

Slice the mushrooms through head and stem and put into a large bowl. Add the shrimp. Combine soy sauce, lemon juice, agi-no-moto or monosodium glutamate, and broth and pour over the mushrooms and shrimp. In a large bowl, steam for 15 minutes; if using 4 small bowls, put 6 shrimp and ¼ of the mushrooms in each and steam 10 minutes.

SERVES 4

LOBSTER

1 lobster, 1¾ to 2 pounds   *Melted butter*
½ teaspoon salt   *Lemon wedges*
2 tablespoons butter

Split the lobster in half lengthwise, remove sac, and crack the claws. Sprinkle with salt and dot with butter. Place on the rack of a steamer and steam until the shell turns red, about 15 minutes. Serve with a small pitcher of melted butter and lemon wedges.

SERVES 2

LOBSTER — HOT OR COLD

4 lobsters (about 1 pound each)
Melted butter or mayonnaise
Lemon wedges

Put the lobsters on a rack or in a pot with an inch of boiling water. Steam until they turn red, about 15 minutes. Split open lengthwise, remove the sac, and serve with a pitcher of melted butter, or cool and serve at room temperature, or chilled, with mayonnaise. Either way, have lemon wedges available.

SERVES 4

LOBSTER TAILS WITH EGGS

3 lobsters or 3 large tails   2 cups water
8 eggs   2 teaspoons salt

Split the lobsters in half lengthwise and steam for 10 minutes. (If using whole lobsters, remove the sac.) When cool enough to handle, pull out the tail meat. Remove meat from large claws. Beat the eggs, add water and salt, and continue to beat. Put the eggs in a serving bowl or deep platter and steam for 8 to 10 minutes, just until set. Place the lobster pieces over the top and steam 10 minutes. It is easier to pull the meat out after steaming the lobster, but you may pull it out raw if you wish. In that case, steam for 12 to 15 minutes until the flesh turns white, placing raw lobster on the eggs. The eggs must be set only enough to support the lobster meat.

SERVES 6

HARD SHELL CRABS
(Sometimes called blue crabs)

---

6 crabs (about 1 pound each)
Melted butter or sauce

Be sure the crabs are alive. Put them into boiling water for a few minutes until their claws stop moving. If they are dirty, scrub them. Put on the rack of a steamer or pot over boiling water, cover tight, and steam for about 20 minutes after the water boils. They should turn orange. Lift out; use tongs so as not to burn your fingers. Serve hot with melted butter on the side, or cold with lemon wedges and mayonnaise, cocktail, or Louis sauce. You need to have nut crackers and picks available. You may want to crack the claws with a hammer before serving.

SERVES 6

The pan used for *paella* in Spain is called *paella*. It is round with slanting sides about 2 inches high and has two handles. You may use any large round pan with sides not over 3 inches high. To steam, you need a cover. However, you can use a piece of foil. Paella in a pan about 13 inches in diameter will serve 6 to 8; a 14-inch pan, 8 to 12. Paella is a not-to-be missed Spanish delight.

PAELLA

1 3½-pound chicken, steamed
1 medium onion, chopped
1 to 2 cloves garlic, minced
¼ cup oil
1½ cups rice
3 cups chicken broth
1 large tomato, peeled and
  chopped
2 teaspoons salt
½ teaspoon pepper
1 teaspoon paprika
¼ teaspoon saffron, dissolved in
  2 tablespoons boiling water

½ pound ham, diced
1 pound medium shrimp, peeled
  and deveined
18 to 24 mussels, scrubbed
12 to 15 clams, scrubbed
1 to 1½ cups shelled peas or 1
  (10-ounce) package frozen,
  thawed
Pimiento, cut in strips, for
  garnish (optional)

Remove the not-overcooked chicken from bones and cut into bite-size pieces, or cut it up, bones and all. Set aside. Stir the onion and garlic into the hot oil, add the rice, and cook and stir until straw-colored. Add 2 cups broth, the tomato, salt, pepper, paprika, and saffron. Cover and cook 10 minutes. Stir in the chicken, shrimp, mussels, and clams. Add the remaining broth, then the peas. Cover and steam 15 minutes until the rice is done and the clams and mussels open. The clams and mussels will give juice. This dish should be moist, not wet. However, you may have to add a little broth or water while steaming. Decorate with pimiento, if you wish. Serve in the pan it was cooked in.

SERVES 8

SEAFOOD PAELLA

¼ *pound salt pork, diced*
2 *cloves garlic, minced*
1 *small onion, minced*
1½ *cups rice*
1 *teaspoon salt*
¼ *teaspoon saffron, dissolved in*
   a little boiling water
1 *medium tomato, chopped*
   (optional)
1 *small green pepper, chopped*
   (optional)

2 *cups clam or chicken broth*
1 *cup water*
1 *pound medium shrimp, peeled*
   and deveined
½ *pound lobster meat, cut up*
½ *pound squid, cleaned and*
   cut into rounds (if available)
½ *pound firm white fish, cut*
   up
24 *mussels, scrubbed*
12 *to 18 clams, scrubbed*

Sauté the salt pork in a *paella* pan until browned, remove the pieces and set aside. Add the garlic, onion, and rice to the fat and stir and cook until straw-colored. Add the salt, saffron, tomato, and green pepper if you wish. Add 1½ cups broth and/or water. Cover and steam 10 minutes. Add the remaining liquid and other ingredients. Stir, cover, and steam 15 minutes. If the rice is not done and the mussels and clams are not open, cook 5 minutes more. If the paella seems dry, add ½ to 1 cup more broth. The dish should be moist, not wet. Stir in the salt pork bits. Serve from the dish it was cooked in.

SERVES 6 TO 8

Poultry, Game and Eggs

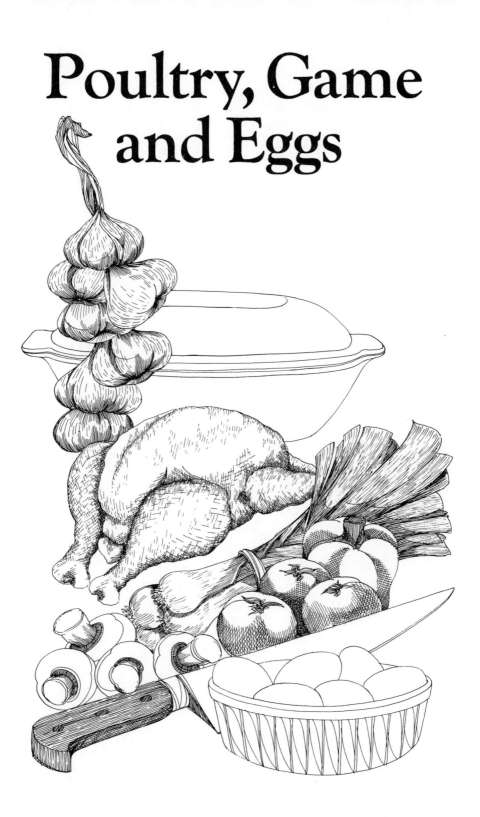

Steaming is the best way to cook a chicken or turkey. Wrapping in foil and cooking in the oven ensures moist tender meat. When you boil, you lose much flavor (and vitamins) in the broth, which you will of course not throw away, but it is of no help to the bird you are cooking. You will have enough concentrated juices in the foil to use for sauce. If a turkey is too big for your steamer, cook it on the grill of your roasting pan. Put a little water (about two inches) on the bottom and cook in sealed foil or covered tight. A bird cooked this way is tender and delicious, and need not come to the table as pale as a ghost if you open the foil and raise the oven temperature to very hot for about the last 20 minutes.

Wild birds tend to be dry, and need the steaming treatment. Rub them with butter, steam for two thirds of the cooking time, and then open the foil to brown them.

If you are planning a turkey or chicken salad or a casserole or other dish using cooked turkey or chicken, you are much better off with a steamed bird than a boiled or roasted one. The meat will come out tender and white, and that's how you want it.

BROILERS

1 3-pound chicken, quartered
3 tablespoons butter
¼ to ½ cup white wine
1 teaspoon salt
¼ teaspoon pepper

2 tablespoons minced chives
2 tablespoons minced parsley
½ teaspoon dried thyme or
   rosemary

Brown the chicken in butter, turning to brown evenly. Add ¼ cup of the wine and the remaining ingredients. Cover and steam for 15 to 20 minutes. If the wine liquid cooks away, add the remaining wine to keep the chicken steaming. The chicken may be steamed on top of the stove or in a 400° oven. Serve with any juices poured over.

SERVES 4

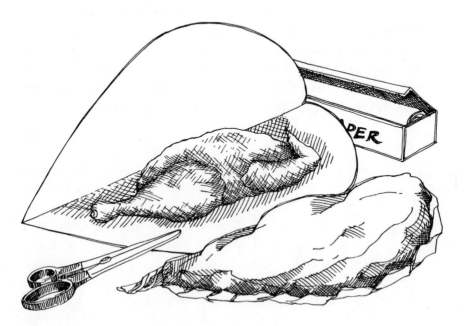

HALF SMALL BROILERS
EN PAPILLOTE

3 2½-pound chickens
Soft butter
1 teaspoon salt
¼ teaspoon pepper
6 teaspoons minced shallots or
    scallions

6 teaspoons chopped
    mushrooms
6 teaspoons minced parsley

Cut the chickens in half and place each half on a piece of generously buttered parchment paper or waxed or brown paper. Sprinkle with salt and pepper. Top each half with a teaspoon of each of the ingredients. Fold the paper tight and make packages from which juices will not leak. Bake in a 400° oven for about 40 minutes or cook on the rack of a steamer. Serve in the paper.

SERVES 6

STEAM-ROAST CHICKEN

1 roasting chicken, 4½ to 5
    pounds
1½ teaspoons salt
3 scallions, cut up

¼ cup water
½ cup dry vermouth
1 to 2 tablespoons flour

Sprinkle the chicken with salt inside and out. Put the chicken in a pot with the scallions, water, and vermouth. Cover tight and steam for 45 minutes. Turn the heat off and let stand for 15 minutes. Place the chicken on a rack over a pan of water in a preheated 450° oven. Cook until browned, about 20 minutes. Meanwhile, remove excess fat from the juices in the pot the chicken was cooked in. Thicken with flour mixed with a little vermouth. Transfer chicken to a hot platter and pass the gravy.

SERVES 6 TO 8

HERBED WHOLE CHICKEN

1 chicken, 3½ to 4½ pounds
1½ teaspoons salt
½ teaspoon pepper
2 medium carrots, sliced
1 large onion, coarsely chopped
1 tablespoon coarsely chopped
  parsley
1 tablespoon chopped fresh or
  ½ teaspoon dried thyme

1 tablespoon chopped fresh or 1
  teaspoon dried basil or
  tarragon
Grated rind of 1 lemon
1 tablespoon lemon juice
1 tablespoon soft butter or olive
  oil

The size of the chicken depends upon the appetites of the diners. Rub the bird with 1 teaspoon salt and ¼ teaspoon pepper. Combine the remaining ingredients except lemon juice and butter. Mix thoroughly and add the remaining salt and pepper. Fill the chicken cavity with the vegetables and sew shut or close tight with poultry pins. Sprinkle the outside of the chicken with lemon juice and brush with butter or oil. Place on a rack and steam for 1 to 1¼ hours, depending upon the size of the chicken. Carve at the table, giving each some of the vegetable stuffing. If you don't have a deep enough steamer, use a deep heavy pot and place the chicken on an inverted pan. Do not let the water in the bottom come up to the chicken. Add more water as needed.

SERVES 4 TO 6

WHOLE CHICKEN WITH LEMON

1 4-pound chicken   ½ teaspoon pepper
Juice of 1 large lemon   2 tablespoons butter
1 teaspoon salt   2 tablespoons chicken broth

Rub the chicken inside and out with lemon, sprinkle with salt and pepper. Place in a dish just large enough to hold the bird. Add the butter and broth and place on the rack of a steamer. Steam for an hour. Serve with the juices

SERVES 6

CHICKEN STUFFED WITH ONIONS

1 3½-pound chicken   Generous pinch saffron
2 tablespoons soft butter   ½ to ¾ pound small white
1 teaspoon salt   onions

Rub the chicken with the butter combined with salt and saffron. Saffron is expensive but adds an interesting flavor to the chicken. Cumin or even ginger may be substituted. Fill the chicken cavity with the peeled onions. Place on the rack of a steamer and cook for an hour.

SERVES 4

CHICKEN WITH GARLIC SAUCE

1 4½-pound chicken
1 teaspoon salt
3 tablespoons butter
2 tablespoons minced onion
3 cloves garlic, minced or
    crushed

1 tablespoon flour
½ teaspoon pepper
1 teaspoon dry or 1 tablespoon
    minced fresh tarragon or
    basil
1 cup chicken broth

Rub the chicken with salt and 1 tablespoon butter. Steam, wrapped in foil, in a 350° oven for an hour. Raise the heat to 450°, open the foil, and cook another 20 minutes. Make the sauce by sautéing the onion and garlic gently in the remaining butter for 1 or 2 minutes. Stir in the flour, pepper, and tarragon. Add the broth slowly while stirring and boil 1 minute. When the chicken is ready, carve it into serving pieces. Add any juices in the foil to the sauce and reheat. Adjust seasoning and pour over the chicken.

SERVES 6

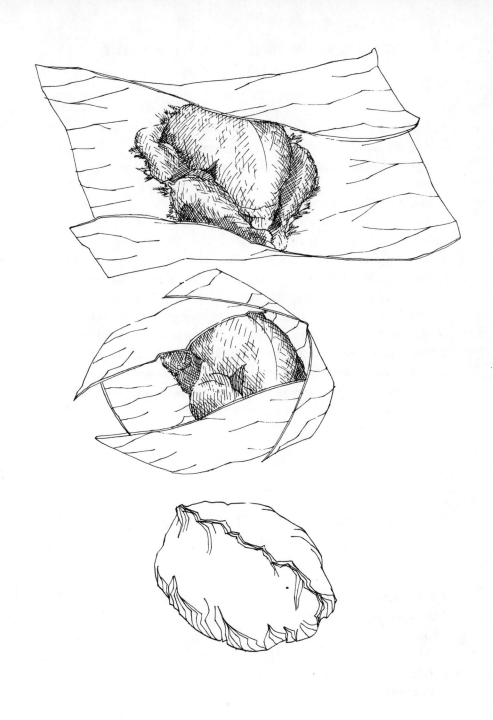

CHICKEN WITH LEEKS OR SCALLIONS

---

1 chicken, 3 to 3½ pounds
1 teaspoon salt
1 large leek or 4 scallions

3 tablespoons white wine or
   vermouth
Cornstarch (optional)

You may leave the chicken whole to be cut later or cut it in half or into pieces. If you want it in small pieces, Chinese fashion, cut through the bones; it is easier to do so after the chicken is cooked. Rub the chicken inside and out with salt and place it in a deep platter or bowl on the rack of a steamer. Steam it for 30 minutes if cut up, longer if whole. In the meantime, sliver the leek or scallions. If using leek, remove some of the green end. When the chicken is done, cut it as you wish and place it on a heated platter. When you remove the chicken, pour the juices in a pan. Add the leek or scallions and the wine and heat; adjust seasoning and pour over the chicken. You may thicken the juices with a little cornstarch mixed with 2 tablespoons of water, if you wish.

SERVES 4

CHICKEN WITH LEMON AND YOGURT

---

1 3½-pound chicken
1 teaspoon salt
1 lemon rind
1 onion, cut up
1 stalk celery, scraped and
   chopped

¼ cup lemon juice
1 cup yogurt or ½ cup sour
   cream

Rub the chicken with salt and the lemon rind. Put the rind inside the bird. Place on the rack of a steamer or steam in a heavy pot. Add the onion, celery, and lemon juice to the water. Steam for about 50 minutes, or until tender. You may have to add a little water while steaming. Remove the chicken and keep it warm. Put the vegetables and about a cup of the liquid into a blender or food processor with yogurt or sour cream. When smooth, taste for seasoning, probably adding lemon juice. If sauce is too thick, add more of the cooking water. You may carve or cut up the bird, place it on a platter, and pour the hot sauce over, or serve it whole and pass the sauce.

SERVES 4

CHICKEN IN A BAG WITH LEMON
(En Papillote)

1 lemon

1 3½-pound chicken

3 sprigs parsley

3 scallions, slivered, or 1 onion,
cut up

1 teaspoon salt

1 tablespoon fresh or ½
teaspoon dried tarragon or
chervil

Grated rind of 1 lemon

2 tablespoons melted butter

4 to 6 new potatoes, peeled

4 to 6 carrots, scraped

4 to 6 small whole white onions

Cut the lemon and squeeze some of the juice and set aside. Cut up the lemon and put it in the cavity of the chicken with parsley and scallions or onion. Rub the chicken outside with the lemon juice, salt, tarragon or chervil, and the grated lemon rind. Pour the butter over. Put the chicken and vegetables in a parchment bag or a buttered brown paper bag. Put in a roaster or baking pan in a 400° oven for 1¼ hours.

SERVES 4

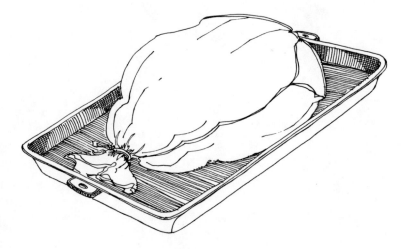

GOLDEN CHICKEN

1 chicken, 5 to 5½ pounds
1 teaspoon salt
¼ teaspoon pepper
¼ cup butter
1 onion, chopped
1 tablespoon lemon juice

4 scallions, chopped fine
1 tablespoon chopped parsley
1 tablespoon flour
2 egg yolks
½ cup cream
Pinch saffron

Rub the chicken with salt and pepper and brown it in 2 tablespoons butter with the onion. When browned, put the chicken on a piece of foil with the pan juices and lemon juice. Set aside the pan, unwashed. Fold the foil to make a tight package and steam the chicken for 1¼ hours in a steamer on top of the stove or in a 375° oven. To make the sauce, brown the scallions in remaining butter, using the pan the chicken was browned in. Add the parsley and stir in the flour. Remove the chicken and pour juices from the foil over the scallions. Simmer 2 or 3 minutes. Mix the egg yolks with the cream and saffron. Stir in and heat, stirring steadily, for 2 minutes. Taste for seasoning. Carve the chicken and heat it in the sauce. Serve with a little of the sauce and pass the rest.

SERVES 6 TO 8

CHICKEN WITH GOLDEN SAUCE

1 roasting chicken, 5 to 5½
  pounds
1 teaspoon salt
¼ teaspoon pepper
2 tablespoons butter
¼ cup chicken broth
SAUCE:
  3 scallions or 6 shallots,
    minced

2 tablespoons butter
2 tablespoons flour or 1
  tablespoon cornstarch
1½ cups chicken broth
2 egg yolks, beaten

Rub the chicken with salt and pepper. Heat the butter and brown the chicken. Transfer the chicken to a large round plate or platter. Add the broth. Steam for 1 to 1½ hours until tender. If using a platter it must of course fit into a pot; or you may put the platter on the rack of a steamer or place the chicken on a piece of foil, turning the foil up at the sides to retain the juices. To make the sauce, sauté the scallions or shallots in butter, add the flour (or cornstarch) and broth, using the liquid from the chicken as part of the 1½ cups of broth. Mix the egg yolks with a little broth and stir in. Carve the chicken at the table and pass the sauce.

SERVES 6 TO 8

CHICKEN IN WHITE WINE
(Coq au Vin Blanc)

1 3½-pound chicken, cut up
1 teaspoon salt
½ teaspoon pepper
2 tablespoons flour
3 tablespoons butter

1 medium onion, minced
1 cup white wine
½ cup chicken broth
½ pound small mushrooms

Rub the pieces of chicken with salt, pepper, and flour and brown them in butter, turning to brown evenly. Stir in the onions. Do this in a casserole or ovenproof dish. Add the wine and ½ cup broth and steam for 40 minutes on top of the stove or in a 400° oven for 60 minutes. Add the mushrooms. If the mushrooms are somewhat large, cut them in half through the stems. Steam 15 minutes more. Serve in the dish the chicken was cooked in.

SERVES 4

CHICKEN IN RED WINE
(Coq au Vin)

¼ pound salt pork, diced
1 3½-pound frying chicken, cut up
2 shallots or 3 scallions, minced
1 clove garlic, minced
1 teaspoon salt

½ teaspoon pepper
½ teaspoon sugar
1 to 2 cups red wine
1 pound small white onions
½ pound small mushrooms

Brown the pork in a casserole or heatproof dish or heavy pot with a tight-fitting lid. Remove the pieces and set aside. Brown the chicken in the pan fat, turning to brown evenly. Add the shallots or scallions, garlic, salt, pepper, sugar, and 1 cup wine. Steam for 20 minutes. Then add the white onions and mushrooms and the pork pieces. Add more wine if needed. Cover and cook 20 minutes. You may cook in a preheated 400° oven for the same length of time. Test to be sure the chicken is tender.

SERVES 4

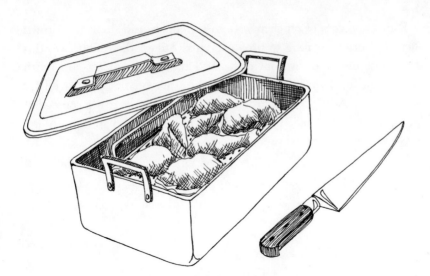

ITALIAN CHICKEN
(Pollo alla Cacciatore)

---

1 3½-pound chicken, cut up
1 teaspoon salt
¼ teaspoon pepper
½ teaspoon sugar
½ teaspoon oregano
1 tablespoon flour
2 tablespoons olive oil

2 onions, sliced thin
1 clove garlic, minced or
* crushed*
1 8-ounce can Italian plum
* tomatoes*
¼ pound mushrooms, sliced
* (optional)*

Rub the chicken with a mixture of salt, pepper, sugar, oregano, and flour. Brown in the oil, turning to brown evenly. Stir in the onions and the garlic; 1 clove is sufficient unless it is very small. Pour in the tomatoes, cover tight, and steam for 30 minutes. Look at the chicken, and if it seems dry add a few tablespoons of water. Steam 15 minutes more. You may add the mushrooms for the last 15 minutes of steaming if you like. This may be cooked in a deep skillet, a Dutch oven, or heavy pot on top of the stove or for 60 minutes in a 400° oven. Any one you use must, of course, have a tight-fitting lid.

SERVES 4

CHICKEN IN BEER
(Huhn in Bier)

1 3½-pound chicken, cut up   *2 tablespoons butter*
1 teaspoon salt   *1 medium onion, diced*
¼ teaspoon pepper   *1 cup beer*
3 tablespoons flour   *½ cup cream (optional)*

Rub the chicken with a mixture of salt, pepper, and 2 tablespoons flour. Brown in the butter, turning to brown evenly. Stir in the onion and cook a minute. This may all be done in a casserole or any pot with a tight-fitting lid. Pour in the beer and steam for 45 minutes on top of the stove or for 60 minutes in a 400° oven. You may add cream and the remaining flour if you wish. It is usual in Germany to bring the chicken to the table in the dish it was cooked in.

SERVES 4

CHICKEN WITH WHITE GRAPES
(Véronique)

1 3½-pound chicken, cut up   *2 tablespoons butter*
1 teaspoon salt   *2 tablespoons water*
¼ teaspoon rosemary or thyme   *½ cup white wine*
1 tablespoon flour   *1 cup seedless white grapes*

Sprinkle the chicken with salt, rosemary or thyme, and flour. Brown in the butter, turning to brown evenly. Do this in a casserole or any heatproof dish with a tight-fitting lid that can go to the table. Add the water and wine. Cover and steam 35 minutes. Add the grapes, cover and steam 15 minutes more.

SERVES 4

CHICKEN IN PORT FROM PORTUGAL

---

1 3½-pound chicken, cut up
2 tablespoons butter or part oil
1 teaspoon salt
¼ teaspoon pepper
2 tablespoons flour
1 clove garlic (optional)

1 tablespoon minced fresh
  coriander or Italian parsley
2 tablespoons water
½ cup port (dry port, white or
  red)
½ cup heavy cream

Brown the chicken in butter, turning to brown evenly. Add the salt, pepper, and flour, and the garlic if you wish. Stir and heat until the flour is straw-colored. Add the coriander or parsley, water, and port. Cover tight and steam for 45 minutes. This can be done on top of the stove or for 60 minutes in a 400° oven. Use a heatproof casserole or other dish with a tight-fitting lid. Stir in the warmed cream and serve from the dish the chicken was cooked in. This may be cooked in a pressure cooker; steam 20 minutes. Add the warm cream after the chicken is ready.

SERVES 4

CHICKEN COUSCOUS

---

1 chicken, 3 to 3½ pounds, cut
  up
1 pound Spanish, Bermuda, or
  red onions, sliced
2 tablespoons oil
2 tablespoons butter
1 teaspoon salt
¼ teaspoon pepper

½ teaspoon cinnamon
2 teaspoons sugar
1 tablespoon minced parsley
2 pinches saffron
¾ cup warm water
½ cup raisins
2 cups couscous

Brown the chicken and half the onions in oil and butter with salt, pepper, cinnamon, sugar, and parsley. Wet the saffron in 2 tablespoons water. Add to the chicken with remaining water and cook for 30 minutes in the bottom of the *couscousière*. Add the remaining onions and cook 20 minutes more. Add the raisins for the last 10 minutes of cooking. Put the couscous grain on a moist cloth on the top rack for the last 20 minutes of cooking. Pile the couscous on a warm platter and surround with the chicken and vegetables. Reduce the juices by boiling and pour them over.

SERVES 4

BROWNED FOWL

---

1 4½-pound fowl
1½ teaspoons salt
¼ teaspoon pepper
2 tablespoons butter or chicken
   or bacon fat

1 teaspoon tarragon or fines
   herbes
Flour (optional)

Rub the fowl with 1 teaspoon salt and the pepper. Cook on the rack of a steamer or in foil in a 350° oven for about 2 hours. If using foil, open the top, pour melted butter over, and sprinkle with tarragon or fines herbes and remaining salt; brown for half an hour in the oven at 450°. If not using foil, place the bird in a pan, add the butter and tarragon or fines herbes, and brown in the oven.at 450° for 25 minutes. Serve with juices poured over or add a little flour mixed with a cup of chicken broth or liquid from the steamer to make gravy.

SERVES 6

PRESSURE-COOKED CHICKEN
WITH DUMPLINGS

---

1 chicken, 5 to 5½ pounds,
   cut into serving pieces
1 tablespoon flour
½ teaspoon salt

1 cup chicken broth
2 onions, minced
Dumplings*
2 tablespoons chopped parsley

Rub the chicken with flour and salt and put it on the rack of a pressure cooker. Pour the broth in, add onions, cover, and steam for 20 minutes at 10 pounds pressure. Cool, remove the chicken to a hot platter, and keep warm. Put the dumpling dough by tablespoonfuls into the pot, not crowding them. They expand. Cover and steam *without pressure valve* for about 8 minutes. Repeat if you haven't used up the dough. Make Dumplings* or Whole Wheat* or Corn Dumplings.* Put on the platter with chicken, pour the juices over, and sprinkle with parsley.

SERVES 6 TO 8

CHINESE CHICKEN WITH GINGER

---

1 3-pound frying chicken
1 tablespoon cornstarch
2 tablespoons soy sauce

2 tablespoons sherry
3 scallions, chopped fine
2 teaspoons chopped ginger

Chop the chicken in 2-inch pieces, through bones and all. Combine the cornstarch, soy sauce, and sherry and add the scallions and ginger. Spread over the chicken in a bowl or deep platter and steam for 40 minutes. Serve in the dish it was steamed in.

SERVES 4

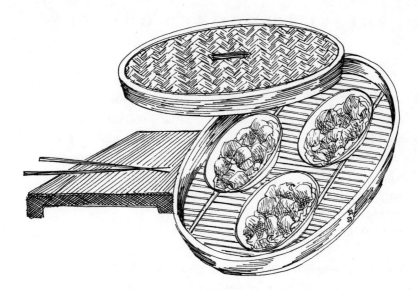

CHINESE CHICKEN
WITH MUSHROOMS

---

1 4½-pound chicken
1 tablespoon soy sauce
2 tablespoons rice wine or
* sherry*
2 tablespoons peanut or
* vegetable oil*

½ teaspoon salt
¼ pound Chinese dried
* mushrooms*
1 scallion, chopped fine
1 (6-ounce) can water
* chestnuts, sliced*

Cut the chicken, bones and all, into bite-size pieces. Mix the soy sauce, wine, oil, and salt and pour over the chicken. Let stand for half an hour, turning once or twice. Meanwhile, soak the mushrooms for half an hour and then cut into slices, discarding tough stems, and combine with the scallion. Mix the vegetables and the chicken and place in a bowl. Put in a pot or steamer and steam over boiling water for 40 minutes after the water in the bottom comes to a boil. Serve in the bowl the chicken was cooked in so it will keep hot and no juice will escape.

SERVES 6

PRESSURE-COOKED CHICKEN FRICASSEE

1 5½-pound hen or roasting
  chicken, cut up
1 cup chicken broth
½ cup dry vermouth or white
  wine
1 teaspoon salt
2 teaspoons minced fresh or ½
  to 1 teaspoon dried tarragon

3 tablespoons prepared mustard
12 small potatoes, peeled
12 small white onions, peeled
½ pound small, whole, or large
  mushrooms, cut in half
Flour (optional)

Put the chicken on the rack of a pressure cooker, pour in the broth and wine, and season with salt and tarragon and mustard. Cover and steam at 10 pounds for 12 minutes for a roasting chicken, 18 minutes if using a stewing hen. Reduce the pressure and add the potatoes and onions. Cover and steam at 10 pounds for 10 minutes. Reduce pressure quickly, open, and put in the mushrooms. Let the liquid simmer, uncovered, for 3 minutes. Remove all to a hot platter. If you have too much liquid, reduce it by boiling it down. You may thicken it slightly with a little flour and water paste if you wish. Good with Dumplings.*

SERVES 8

CHICKEN WITH DRIED MUSHROOMS

1 chicken, 3 to 3½ pounds
2 ounces dried mushrooms,
  soaked and cut up
1 tablespoon minced fresh
  ginger

3 scallions, slivered
1 tablespoon soy sauce
3 tablespoons sherry
Flour or cornstarch (optional)

Steam the chicken for 20 minutes. Remove and let it cool. Chop into pieces, 1 to 1½ inches, through bone and flesh. Or leave the chicken whole if you wish to carve at the table. Place in a heatproof serving bowl or casserole. Add the remaining ingredients. Cover with a lid or foil and bake at 400° for about 60 minutes. You may steam on top of the stove for 45 minutes if you prefer. Be sure to serve with all of the liquid, which may be thickened with a little flour or cornstarch paste.

SERVES 4

ORANGE CHICKEN WITH HONEY

1 3½-pound chicken, cut up
2 teaspoons grated orange rind
1 teaspoon salt
Pinch cloves

3 oranges
2 tablespoons butter
½ cup boiling chicken broth
¼ cup honey

Rub the chicken with orange rind, salt, and cloves. Peel the oranges, cutting away all the white pith. Section the oranges, saving the juice. Brown the chicken in butter in a casserole or similar dish with a tight-fitting lid. Add the juice from the oranges; you should have about half a cup. Cover and steam for 30 minutes. Combine the boiling broth with honey, add to the chicken, and steam 20 minutes more. Add the orange sections and cover the pot. Turn off the heat and let stand for a few minutes to heat the oranges. You will have extra liquid, which can be passed separately.

SERVES 4

CHICKEN WITH YOGURT

1 3½-pound chicken, cut up
2 cups yogurt
2 scallions, chopped fine

1 clove garlic, minced
2 tablespoons lemon juice
Grated rind of 1 lemon

Put the chicken and the yogurt into a pot. Turn to coat evenly. Add the scallions and garlic and steam for 30 minutes over low heat or steam in the oven at 400°. Add the lemon juice and rind and steam 20 minutes longer. If the chicken becomes too dry while steaming, add a little water.

SERVES 4

CHICKEN BREASTS IN FOIL

6 half chicken breasts
2 bay leaves, broken
1 cup chicken broth
1 tablespoon minced parsley
2 tablespoons minced chives
¼ teaspoon thyme

¼ teaspoon tarragon
1 teaspoon salt
¼ teaspoon pepper
¼ cup chopped mushrooms
  (optional)

Place each breast on a piece of foil. Combine all of the remaining ingredients and divide it among the chicken breasts. Fold the foil over each breast envelope fashion, being very sure no liquid can escape. Bake at 375° for 40 minutes or put on the rack of a steamer. Serve in the foil so each may open his own package and enjoy the aroma and get all of the juices.

SERVES 6

CHICKEN AND MUSHROOMS

2 chicken breasts
1 teaspoon salt
¼ teaspoon pepper

6 to 8 ounces fresh mushrooms,
  chopped
1 tablespoon oil

Remove skin and bones from the chicken breasts and chop the meat fine or grind not too fine in a food processor. Combine with 1 teaspoon salt and the pepper and spread onto a flat dish. Steam for 20 minutes. Combine the mushrooms with oil and a little salt and spread over the chicken. Steam for 10 minutes more. Serve in the dish it was steamed in. Good on toast or with rice or noodles.

SERVES 4

CHICKEN WITH BANANAS

2 3½-pound frying chickens
1 teaspoon salt
1 tablespoon soy sauce
4 bananas

2 tablespoons butter
Ti leaves or foil
1 cup chicken broth

Quarter the chicken and sprinkle with salt and soy sauce. Cut the bananas in half lengthwise and then cut them again into quarters. Sauté for a few minutes in butter. Place chicken on ti leaves or foil in a baking dish or in individual ovenproof dishes. Place pieces of banana on top. Divide the broth and pour over each portion. Fold leaves or foil over and bake at 350° for 45 minutes.

SERVES 8

CHICKEN WITH EGGS AND HAM
ORIENTAL STYLE

*2 chicken breasts, cut into thin
    slices*
*½ pound ham, cut into thin
    slices*
2 tablespoons shoyu or soy sauce

2 tablespoons sherry or sake
6 eggs
½ teaspoon salt
2 tablespoons chicken broth

Place the chicken and ham in a bowl. Pour 1 tablespoon shoyu and the sherry or sake over. Let stand a few minutes, tossing once or twice. Beat the eggs with salt, chicken broth, and remaining shoyu or soy sauce. Pour the egg mixture over the chicken and steam 20 minutes. If you wish to use separate bowls, divide the chicken and ham mixture into the bowls, pour the eggs over, and steam 15 minutes more.

SERVES 6

JAPANESE CHICKEN AND HAM

*1 frying chicken, 3 to 3½
    pounds*
*½ pound ham, cut about ½
    inch thick*

2 teaspoons Japanese soy sauce
1 tablespoon peanut oil
1 tablespoon minced scallions
1 tablespoon minced parsley

Cut the chicken into 2-inch pieces through bones and all. Cut the ham into ¾-inch squares. Arrange the chicken and ham in alternate layers in a bowl or deep platter. Pour a mixture of soy sauce and oil over and sprinkle with scallions and parsley. Steam for 40 minutes.

SERVES 4

JAPANESE CHICKEN WITH EGGS

10 ounces fresh or 6 ounces
    dried mushrooms, sliced
2 chicken breasts, cut into
    bite-size pieces
1 tablespoon shoyu or soy sauce
2 tablespoons sherry

6 eggs
½ teaspoon salt
2 tablespoons chicken broth
¼ pound young spinach or
    watercress

If using dried mushrooms, soak them in warm water for half an hour before slicing; remove any hard pieces of stem. Combine the mushrooms and chicken in a bowl. Pour shoyu or soy sauce and sherry over and let marinate for about an hour, turning once or twice to coat all sides of the chicken. Beat the eggs with salt and broth and pour over the chicken. Steam for 15 minutes. Remove tough stems from spinach and cut it into strips about 1 inch long. If using watercress, remove tough stems and chop coarsely. Put over the eggs for another 5 minutes of steaming.

SERVES 6

CHICKEN WITH HAM

2 chicken breasts
½ pound ham
1 teaspoon Dijon mustard
1 tablespoon sherry

2 tablespoons chicken broth
½ teaspoon sugar
½ teaspoon salt
1 teaspoon tarragon

Dice the chicken flesh and ham in similar-size pieces. Mix the mustard with the remaining ingredients. Put the chicken-ham mixture in a heatproof bowl or casserole and pour the mustard mixture over. Place on the rack of a steamer and steam for 20 minutes. Adjust seasoning. Serve in the bowl it was cooked in.

SERVES 4

CHICKEN IN VERMOUTH

6 half chicken breasts or legs or
   some of each
1 teaspoon salt
½ teaspoon pepper
1 teaspoon tarragon

2 tablespoons butter or oil
¼ cup dry vermouth
¼ cup sweet vermouth
Flour (optional)

Rub the chicken with salt, pepper, and tarragon and place on lightly greased foil. Make 6 individual foil packages. Or, especially if using a mixture of white and dark meat, place in one package. Pour the melted butter or oil and vermouth over. Seal tight and steam about 40 minutes in a steamer or 400° oven. Serve with the juices, which you may thicken with a little flour and water paste if you wish.

SERVES 6

CHICKEN AND BEAN SPROUTS

2 chicken breasts
2 cups sliced or chopped celery
2 cups bean sprouts
¼ cup soy sauce
1 cup chicken broth

1 teaspoon salt
½ teaspoon pepper
1 teaspoon sugar
1 tablespoon cornstarch
¼ cup water

Slice the chicken thin. Place the chicken with the remaining ingredients, except the cornstarch and water, in a heavy pot. Cover tight and steam for 20 minutes. Blend the cornstarch with ¼ cup water, add to the juices, and let boil for 2 minutes. Serve the chicken with all juices poured over.

SERVES 4

CHICKEN-STUFFED WON TON

Chinese won ton skins
  (available in packages in
  Chinese markets)
1 large chicken breast, boned
  and skinned
1 clove garlic, chopped
1 tablespoon cornstarch

½ teaspoon salt
¼ teaspoon pepper
1 teaspoon soy sauce
2 egg whites
2 tablespoons sherry
1 to 2 tablespoons water

Cut up the chicken and place in a food processor or blender with the remaining ingredients. Add water as you run the machine to make a paste. Place a layer of won ton skins on a flat surface and put a teaspoon of filling on each. Fold over and pinch shut. Wet your fingers as you seal the won tons. Continue until all of the filling is used. Place on the rack of a steamer or a bamboo steamer layer and steam for 7 to 8 minutes.

SERVES 8 TO 10

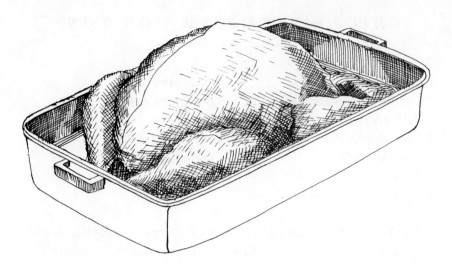

STEAM-ROAST STUFFED TURKEY

1 10-pound turkey
Soft butter or margarine
Stuffing*

Wipe the bird with a damp cloth if you wish; do not wash it. Pull out any loose fat from inside. Use any of the suggested Stuffings.* Stuff the body and neck cavities loosely. You will need 4½ to 5 cups of stuffing. A good rule is a little less than ½ cup of stuffing for each pound of poultry. Brush the skin with a little soft butter or margarine and place the turkey on a large sheet of heavy foil, fold the foil up over the breast, turn up the ends, and fold or crumple it so juices cannot escape. Steam at 425° for about 1½ hours. Open the foil at the top so the bird will brown and cook 30 minutes longer. The total cooking time is quite a lot less than for roasted turkey and will produce a more moist bird. A 15-pound turkey will take 3 hours; a 20-pound one, 3½ hours total cooking time.

SERVES 10

ROAST TURKEY IN FOIL

1 turkey, about 10 pounds
2 teaspoons salt
Soft butter

Wipe the turkey with a damp cloth. Remove any loose fat from inside the bird. Sprinkle inside and out with salt and brush the outside with a little butter. Wrap securely in foil, folding so no juices can escape. Place breast side up in a roasting pan and steam at 400° for about 2¼ hours. Keep a little water in the bottom of the roaster. If you are using the turkey in a casserole or salad, do not brown it. If you are serving it from the oven, open the foil for the last half hour of cooking so it will brown and the skin will be crisp. You will have juices to use for gravy or in a turkey dish. A little of the concentrated liquid is good to thin and flavor mayonnaise for turkey salad.

SERVES ABOUT 12

CORNISH GAME HENS

4 Cornish game hens (about
  1¼ pounds each, preferably
  fresh)
1 cup chicken broth
¼ cup white wine
1 small onion, minced
½ teaspoon blended poultry
  herbs or tarragon

½ teaspoon salt
Pinch sugar
1 tablespoon flour
Minced fresh tarragon or
  parsley

Fresh game hens are much tenderer than frozen. If using frozen, thaw them. Put the hens in a casserole or heatproof dish with the remaining ingredients except the flour and tarragon or parsley. Cover tight and steam for 30 minutes. Remove the hens. When they are cool enough to handle, remove the skin and cut the hens in halves or quarters. Add the flour, mixed with a little water, to the liquid and boil for 2 or 3 minutes. Adjust the seasoning. Return the hens to the pot and cover tight. Put into a 350° oven for 20 minutes. Sprinkle with fresh tarragon and/or parsley and serve in the dish they were cooked in.

SERVES 6 TO 8

POTTED SQUABS

6 squabs
2 teaspoons salt
½ teaspoon pepper
¼ cup melted butter

1 cup chicken broth or part
white wine
Flour (optional)

Wipe the squabs with a damp cloth. Add salt and pepper to the butter and brush on the outside of the birds. Place in a pot or casserole with ½ cup of liquid. Cover tight and steam for 45 minutes. Add the remaining broth and season the liquid to taste. Cover and steam half an hour. You may thicken the juices with a little flour and water paste.

SERVES 6

SQUABS WITH PEAS

Proceed as for Potted Squabs,* adding 3 cups of fresh or 2 (10-ounce) packages frozen peas, thawed, and a generous pinch of sugar. Add fresh peas for the last 20 minutes of cooking. Add frozen peas, thawed, for 12 minutes.

SERVES 6

ORANGE DUCK

1 duck, 4 to 5 pounds
1 tablespoon salt
1 teaspoon coarsely ground
 pepper
2 tablespoons grated orange
 rind

½ cup orange marmalade
2 tablespoons Grand Marnier or
 any orange liqueur

Wipe the duck. Combine salt, pepper, and orange rind and wipe inside and out with the mixture. Let stand several hours before cooking. Steam until tender, about 1½ to 2 hours. Transfer to a hot platter and let stand 15 minutes. Meanwhile, melt the orange marmalade with ½ cup water from the steamer. Add any juice that has dripped onto the platter, add the liqueur, heat, and pour over the duck.

SERVES 4

DUCK ORIENTAL STYLE

¼ pound ham, cut into ¼-inch
 slivers
1 cup bamboo shoots, cut into
 ¼-inch pieces
2 scallions, slivered

1 teaspoon chopped fresh ginger
2 teaspoons soy sauce
1 4-pound duck
1 teaspoon salt

Combine the ham, bamboo shoots, scallions, ginger, and soy sauce. Put some inside the duck and spread the rest over. Steam in a bowl for 1½ to 2 hours. Sprinkle with salt and serve with all the ingredients and all the liquid.

SERVES 4

PINEAPPLE DUCK

1 4½-pound duck
1 (8-ounce) can sliced
  pineapple

1 teaspoon salt
1 tablespoon cornstarch
1 tablespoon sherry or sake

Wipe the duck and steam for 1½ hours, or until tender. Drain the pineapple and pour the juice in a saucepan. Add the salt and blend the cornstarch with a little water; pour into the saucepan. Simmer until thickened. Meanwhile either cut the duck into bite-size pieces, through bones and all, or slice the meat into ½-inch slices. Either way, place on a heated platter and keep warm. Cut the pineapple slices into 3 or 4 pieces each, place on the duck, add the sherry to the hot sauce, pour over the duck.

SERVES 4

CHINESE STUFFED DUCK

1 5-pound duck
1 teaspoon salt
6 to 8 dried mushrooms
½ pound pork, ground
1 (8-ounce) can water
  chestnuts

1 teaspoon minced fresh ginger
1 tablespoon sherry
1 cup cooked rice
1 tablespoon soy sauce

Wipe the duck and sprinkle with salt; set aside. Soak the mushrooms in water just to cover for half an hour. Remove tough stems and chop the mushrooms coarsely, saving the water. Combine the remaining ingredients with the mushrooms. If the stuffing is too dry, moisten with some of the mushroom water. Fill the duck and skewer or sew the opening. Steam either in a bowl or in a steamer for 2 hours. Carve at the table, cutting into ½-inch-thick slices.

SERVES 6

DUCK WITH MUSHROOMS
AND ALMONDS

---

1 4-pound duck
½ cup chicken broth
¼ cup sherry
1 teaspoon salt

¾ pound mushrooms, sliced
½ cup blanched slivered
  almonds

Wipe the duck and score the meat with the point of a sharp knife. Place in a deep heatproof bowl with the broth, sherry, and salt. Place the bowl in boiling water in a large pot; the water should come about a third of the way up the bowl. Cover the pot and steam for 1½ hours. Replace the water as necessary. Remove the duck, put the mushrooms and almonds in the bowl, and replace the duck. Cover the pot and steam 20 minutes. An old duck may take a little longer. Carve at the table and pass hot juices with the mushrooms and almonds.

SERVES 4

GOOSE IN RED WINE

1 goose, 5 to 5½ pounds
1 large Bermuda onion, peeled
  and sliced
1½ teaspoons salt
1 tablespoon chopped fresh or 1
  teaspoon dried basil,
  tarragon, or thyme

1 cup red wine
Flour or cornstarch (optional)

Cut the goose into serving pieces and remove as much fat as possible. Heat some of the fat in the bottom of a pressure cooker. You need about 3 tablespoons. Brown the goose in the fat, turning to brown evenly. Add the onion and stir and brown. Add the remaining ingredients, except flour or cornstarch. Steam at 15 pounds for 15 minutes or at 10 pounds for 20 minutes. Reduce pressure at once and transfer the goose to a warm deep platter or bowl; keep it warm. Scoop off as much fat as possible from the juices. Thicken, if you wish, with a little flour or cornstarch and water paste. Pour over the goose or pass separately.

SERVES 6

White-meat game birds such as pheasants, partridge, and grouse tend to be dry, whether shot or from a bird farm. Shot ducks and geese, which are dark meat, are also much drier than domestic ones. They are all improved by being steamed for part of the cooking time and then browned. Never cook delicate game birds in a pressure cooker.

GROUSE, BABY PHEASANT, OR PARTRIDGE

4 birds
1 teaspoon salt
¼ teaspoon pepper
4 pieces lemon rind

4 teaspoons butter
8 slices bacon or thin slices salt pork

Wipe the birds and rub with salt and pepper. Put a piece of lemon rind and 1 teaspoon butter in the cavity of each. Wrap in bacon or salt pork and place each on a square of foil. You may put 2 on one piece if you wish unless you are serving separately in the foil. Fold over tight and steam at 400° for 30 minutes, 40 if you know the birds are old. Open the foil and brown at 450° for about 10 minutes, until the bacon is crisp and the birds browned. Serve with all the juices. If the birds are large (1½ to 2 pounds), cut them in half after cooking.

SERVES 4 TO 8

GUINEA HENS

(They are distantly related to pheasants and have a slightly gamey flavor.)

3 guinea hens, about 2½ pounds each
2 teaspoons salt
Soft butter

Wipe the birds, sprinkle with salt, and rub generously with soft butter. Place breast side up on a piece of foil. Fold the foil around the birds, either in one package or three. Be sure to secure the edges of the foil so no juices can escape. Put into a 400° oven for 60 minutes. Raise temperature to 450° and open the foil for the last 20 minutes of cooking to brown the hens and to crisp the skin. Or you may cut the hens in half. Wrap each half in a piece of buttered foil and steam for 45 minutes. Open the foil and put under the broiler for the last 15 minutes of cooking.

SERVES 6

Quail are small, delicate, and delicious. Wipe the birds and rub with a little salt and pepper and put a piece of butter inside each. You may also rub the breast with a little soft butter or brown the birds gently in butter. Place in a covered pot with ½ inch of water or chicken broth or put on the rack of a steamer. Cook for half an hour. You may steam them in foil, adding a tablespoon of broth or white wine to the foil for each 2 birds. The usual serving is 2 quail per person.

QUAIL WITH LETTUCE

12 quail
2 ounces salt pork, cubed
6 slices bacon or 12 small thin
    slices salt pork

1 head iceberg lettuce, shredded
½ cup broth

Wipe the quail with a damp cloth. Place a small piece of pork inside each bird. Put a half slice of bacon or a pork slice over the breast and fasten in place with thread or with toothpicks. Place on a bed of half the lettuce. Add the broth. Cover and steam for 30 minutes. Add the remaining lettuce, and a little more broth if necessary (it should not be, as the lettuce makes liquid). Steam another 20 minutes. Serve with juices poured over.

SERVES 6

WILD DUCKS

A canvasback or mallard will usually serve 2 people. However, teal, the smallest of the wild ducks, will serve only one. To steam ducks, leave whole or cut in half. Brown in a little butter in a pot. Sprinkle with salt and pepper and add broth or water to a depth of about ½ inch in the bottom of the pot. Cover and steam for 35 minutes. Add ½ cup of red wine, Madeira, or sherry, cover and steam 20 minutes more. If you like wild ducks rare, steam a total of 30 minutes.

EGGS

Eggs take kindly to steaming, however you want them cooked, from simple boiled, shirred, poached, or scrambled to an elaborate soufflé.

There are two simple rules to follow: First, try to get fresh eggs and, second, have them at room temperature before cooking.

POACHED EGGS

Poached eggs are usually steamed in an egg poacher, which has little pockets to hold each egg. However, you can poach in buttered ramekins or custard cups; some will hold one egg, some two. In every case, sprinkle with a little salt and butter. For a change, add a drop or two of Worcestershire sauce, Angostura bitters, or Tabasco sauce to each egg. Steam only until the white is set, about 3 minutes.

BOILED EGGS

Steamed eggs are more tender and cook more evenly than those cooked in deep water. The timing is slightly different.

The popular 3-minute egg takes 5 on the rack of a steamer, while hard-cooked eggs need about 20 minutes. Experiment for the time of soft-cooked eggs to get them exactly as you want them.

SCRAMBLED EGGS

---

8 eggs
1 teaspoon salt
¼ teaspoon pepper

2 tablespoons warm water
(optional)

Beat the eggs with the remaining ingredients in a heatproof bowl. Milk may be substituted for water but the water makes lighter eggs. Steam on a rack or propped up in a pot with an inch or two of boiling water in the bottom. Be sure the water doesn't boil over the rim of the bowl. Steam 3 minutes, stir, and steam 3 minutes and stir again. The eggs should be quite moist. If you want them more firm, steam an extra 2 minutes. Stir before serving.

SERVES 4

EGGS WITH SHERRY

---

8 eggs
1 teaspoon salt

2 tablespoons warm water
2 tablespoons sherry

Beat the eggs with remaining ingredients. Place in bowl on a steamer tray or in a pot with boiling water in the bottom. Steam for about 6 minutes or until the eggs are set. Be sure the water doesn't overboil the rim of the bowl. Serve the eggs from the bowl.

SERVES 4

Variations

EGGS WITH CHICKEN

Add 1 cup of diced cooked chicken to Scrambled Eggs* and substitute chicken broth for the water.

EGGS WITH BACON

Fry 3 strips of bacon until crisp. Dry on paper toweling and crumble into Scrambled Eggs.*

EGGS WITH MINCED PORK

Add 1 cup minced cooked pork, 2 scallions, chopped, and 1 tablespoon soy sauce to Scrambled Eggs.*

EGGS WITH HAM

8 eggs
1 cup or 3 tablespoons water
1 teaspoon salt

3 tablespoons minced ham
1 tablespoon minced parsley

Break the eggs into a heatproof bowl. If you want the consistency of custard, stir in 1 cup water and remaining ingredients and steam for 20 minutes in the bowl. If you want the consistency of scrambled eggs, beat the eggs until fluffy, add 3 tablespoons warm water, and the remaining ingredients. Steam for 3 minutes, stir, and repeat twice. If you want them soft, 9 minutes should be enough.

They will continue to cook in the hot bowl away from the steam.

SERVES 4

EGGS WITH MUSHROOMS

8 eggs
4 tablespoons water
¼ pound fresh or 1 ounce dried
 mushrooms
1 tablespoon grated onion

2 tablespoons minced parsley
1 teaspoon salt
½ teaspoon pepper
2 tablespoons butter

Beat the eggs and water in a heatproof bowl. If using dried mushrooms, soak for 30 minutes in hot water. Remove and discard stems and cut the mushrooms fine. Add mushrooms and remaining ingredients except butter to the eggs. Steam for about 10 minutes, stirring several times. Stir in the butter just before serving.

SERVES 4

CHINESE EGGS

(These are rather like a custard and are served as a side dish.)

6 eggs
1 cup chicken broth or milk,
   heated and cooled
½ to 1 teaspoon salt

¼ teaspoon pepper
1 scallion, minced
2 teaspoons soy sauce

Beat the eggs lightly (not frothy) in a heatproof bowl. Add the broth or milk at room temperature. Broth should have been boiled, the milk just brought to a boil. Use ½ teaspoon salt with broth, 1 teaspoon with milk. Add the scallion and steam for about 20 minutes without stirring. Test with a toothpick; if it does not come out clean, steam 5 minutes longer. The result should be smooth and custardy. Sprinkle with soy sauce.

SERVES 6

EGGS WITH PORK

8 eggs
½ pound pork, minced
1 teaspoon salt

1 teaspoon soy sauce
½ cup broth
1 scallion, minced

Break the eggs into a heatproof bowl and stir lightly. Add the remaining ingredients and stir to mix thoroughly. Steam for 20 minutes. Serve at once.

SERVES 4

CUSTARD EGGS WITH SHRIMP OR CLAMS

8 eggs
1½ cups water
1 teaspoon salt
2 tablespoons sherry

½ pound shrimp, steamed and
    chopped fine, or 1 (6-ounce)
    can minced clams, puréed
2 scallions, minced

Beat the eggs, water, salt, and sherry lightly together in a heatproof bowl. Add the minced shrimp and scallions. If using clams, purée in a blender or processor, add to the eggs with the scallions, and stir well. Steam for 20 minutes. If a toothpick does not come out clean, steam 5 minutes more. The custard will continue to cook away from the steam.

SERVES 4

CHEESE EGG PUDDING

¼ cup butter
5 eggs, separated
½ cup grated Swiss cheese

¼ cup flour
½ teaspoon salt

Cream the butter and stir in the egg yolks. Add the cheese and mix well. Stir in the flour. Add salt to the egg whites and beat until stiff. Fold into the cheese mixture. Spoon into a greased mold, cover, and steam gently for 40 to 45 minutes. Unmold onto a heated plate or platter.

SERVES 6 AS A SIDE DISH; 4 AS A COURSE

PARMESAN CHEESE PUDDING

¼ *cup butter*
½ *cup flour*
1 *cup hot milk*

4 *eggs, separated*
¾ *cup Parmesan cheese*

Melt the butter (do not brown), stir in the flour, and add the milk gradually while stirring. Cook and stir 5 minutes. Cool. Add the beaten egg yolks and cheese. Beat the egg whites until stiff and fold in. Pour into a buttered mold or bowl, cover, and steam for about 35 minutes. If you put it in a pot, do not let the water come more than a third of the way up the mold. Add water as needed. Unmold to serve.

SERVES 4

Meat

Steam is a blessing in these days when meat is so expensive. You don't need prime cuts for steam cookery. The cheaper cuts come out of the steamer fork-tender and succulent. You know that is true of a pot roast, which is in fact not roasted but steamed. It is also true of Italian Bollito Misto (Mixed Boil)* and New England Boiled Dinner,* both of which are much better steamed. So are braised lamb shanks and every kind of stew.

POT ROAST

1 4-pound piece of lean beef
(round, chuck, or sirloin tip)
2 teaspoons salt
¼ teaspoon pepper

1 medium onion, minced
¾ cup Burgundy-type red wine
Cornstarch (optional)

Rub the beef with salt and pepper. Place in a heavy pot. Add the onion and wine. Cover tight and put into a 400° oven for an hour. Reduce heat to 350° and cook about 1½ hours more. You may thicken the juices with a little cornstarch made into a paste with water.

SERVES 6

BEEF POT ROAST IN A PRESSURE COOKER

1 4½-pound beef roast (rump or round)
2 cloves garlic, slivered
2 ounces salt pork, slivered or diced

1 teaspoon salt
¼ teaspoon pepper
2 tablespoons oil
1 cup beef broth or consommé
Flour

Make small cuts in the roast with the tip of a sharp knife and insert a sliver of garlic and a piece of salt pork. Rub the meat with salt and pepper. Heat the oil in a pressure cooker and brown the meat, turning to brown evenly. Add the broth or consommé and steam at 10 pounds for 40 minutes. Let the pressure fall slowly. Lift the roast onto a warm platter and thicken the juices with a little flour and water paste. Taste for seasoning.

SERVES 6 TO 8

POT ROAST WITH PRUNES

5 to 5½ pounds beef roast (round, rump, or sirloin)
1 teaspoon salt
½ teaspoon pepper
¼ cup oil

4 medium onions, sliced
1 cup water
½ cup red wine
1 pound prunes
Flour (optional)

Rub the roast with salt and pepper and brown in the oil in a heavy pot. Add the onions and stir and brown them. Add the water and wine. Cover and steam for 1½ hours, turning the meat several times. Meanwhile, soak the prunes in a little water. Add to the roast (with the water if more liquid is needed). Cover and steam another 40 minutes or until tender. Remove the pot roast to a hot platter and surround with the prunes. Thicken the liquid with a little flour and water paste if you want a thicker gravy.

SERVES 10

POT ROAST IN FOIL

1 piece of beef, 3 to 3½
   pounds (round or sirloin tip)
1 onion, minced
1 teaspoon salt
¼ teaspoon pepper

⅓ cup water
½ cup red wine
2 tablespoons Worcestershire
   sauce
2 tablespoons flour

Place the meat on a large piece of heavy foil. Fold the foil up and add remaining ingredients except the flour. Fold the foil shut, closing it tight so no juice can escape. Bake at 400° for about 2½ hours or until tender. Make a paste of the flour and a little water in a saucepan. When ready to serve, put the meat on a platter and keep it warm. Pour all of the liquid into the flour mixture and heat and stir until thickened. Add a little red wine if you don't have enough gravy. Adjust seasoning. Pour a little gravy over the meat and pass the rest.

SERVES 6

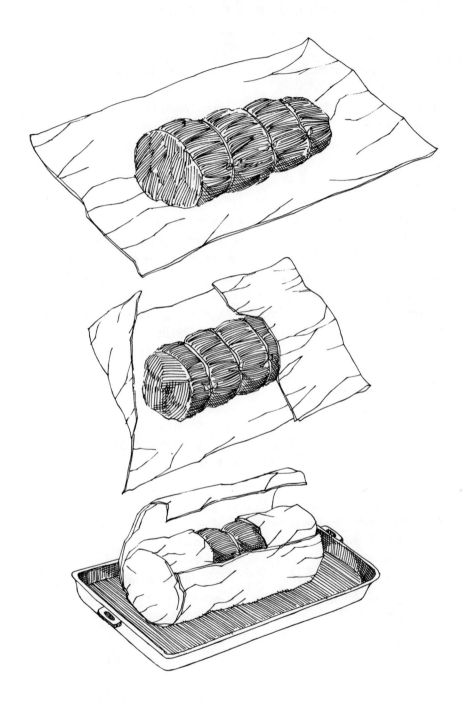

SPICY POT ROAST

---

1 3-pound piece of beef rump,
  boneless
2 tablespoons butter
1 cup vinegar
2 cups water
10 cloves
1 bay leaf

½ teaspoon oregano
2 teaspoons salt
½ teaspoon pepper
1 teaspoon sugar
Grated rind of 1 lemon
1 to 2 tablespoons flour

Place the beef in a bowl with all of the remaining ingredients except the flour. Let stand 12 hours, or overnight, in the marinade. The beef should be turned several times. Place the meat in a heavy deep pot with ½ cup of the marinade. Cover and steam for about 2 hours or until tender. You will have to add a little more of the marinade as needed. You may thicken the gravy with the flour made into a thin paste with some of the marinade.

SERVES 6

SAUERBRATEN IN A PRESSURE COOKER

---

1 4½-pound piece of beef
  (round or chuck)
1 teaspoon salt
1 teaspoon coarse pepper
¼ pound salt pork, sliced thin
2 cups vinegar
2 cups water

1 large onion, cut up
⅓ cup sugar
8 gingersnaps
3 tablespoons pork or other fat
1 cup sour cream
Flour (optional)

Rub the meat with the salt and pepper. Place the pork around the meat and fasten with skewers or toothpicks. Place in a deep bowl with the remaining ingredients except the fat and sour cream. Let stand in the refrigerator for a day or two, turning several times. Remove the meat, pat dry, and brown in the fat in the pressure cooker, turning to brown evenly. Add 2 cups of the marinade. Steam at 15 pounds for 45 minutes. Cool at once. Remove the meat to a warm platter. Add the sour cream to the liquid. If you wish to make gravy thicker add a little flour and water paste before adding the sour cream.

SERVES 6 TO 8

IRISH STEAK AND KIDNEY STEW

3 pounds stewing beef, cut into
   1-inch cubes
1 teaspoon salt
½ teaspoon pepper
2 tablespoons flour

3 medium onions, sliced
1 cup water
2 beef kidneys
1 tablespoon chopped parsley

Trim the beef and roll in a mixture of salt, pepper, and flour. Add onions and put into a heavy pot or casserole with a tight-fitting lid. Add the water, cover, and steam for 1½ hours until the beef is almost tender. Check the water level. Slice the kidneys, removing the hard center core. Add to the pot and steam for 20 minutes. The kidney will be tough if you cook it longer. If you prefer, you may add the kidneys for the entire cooking time. This adds flavor to the stew but the kidney itself is less tasty. Garnish with chopped parsley.

SERVES 6

BEEF WITH BROCCOLI

1½ pounds boneless beef, fillet
   or sirloin
1 teaspoon salt
¼ teaspoon pepper

2 tablespoons sherry
1 tablespoon flour
1 cup sliced broccoli

Cut the beef into thin slices about 2 inches long. Place on a small deep platter that will fit into a steamer. Sprinkle with ½ teaspoon salt and the pepper. Mix the sherry with the flour. Pour it over the beef and mix thoroughly. Scrape the stems of the broccoli and slice it thin. Place over the beef. Sprinkle with the remaining salt and steam for 20 to 30 minutes. The steaming time depends upon the cut of beef used. Fillet takes no more than 20 minutes.

SERVES 4

GINGER BEEF

2½ pounds lean beef, sliced
   thin
2 tablespoons minced fresh
   ginger
3 scallions, coarsely chopped

2 tablespoons sherry
1 teaspoon salt
½ teaspoon pepper
Minced parsley

Combine the beef with the remaining ingredients except the parsley. Stir well and place in a dish. Steam for about 20 minutes. Sprinkle with parsley and serve in the bowl it was cooked in.

SERVES 6

BEEF STROGANOFF

2½ pounds lean beef (fillet, top
  sirloin, or top round)
1 teaspoon salt
¼ teaspoon pepper
1 teaspoon paprika
3 tablespoons butter
2 medium onions, sliced
½ pound mushrooms,
  quartered if large

½ cup beef broth or water
1 tablespoon flour
1 tablespoon Worcestershire
  sauce
1 to 1½ cups sour cream or
  yogurt

Cut the beef into strips about 2½ inches long, removing excess fat. Sprinkle with salt, pepper, and paprika. Brown in the butter in a heavy pot, turning to brown evenly. Add the onions and mushrooms. Stir and cook 2 minutes. Add ⅓ cup broth, cover tight and steam for 20 to 25 minutes until the beef is tender. Remove to a warm platter. Skim the fat from the liquid. Mix the flour and Worcestershire sauce with the remaining broth. Stir in and simmer for a few minutes. Remove from heat and stir in the cream. The amount depends upon how creamy you want the sauce. Spoon the sauce over the stew.

SERVES 6

BEEF STEW

3 pounds beef stew meat, cubed
1 large onion, sliced
3 stalks celery, scraped and cut
 up
6 potatoes, peeled and cut up
2 tablespoons tapioca

½ cup tomato juice
½ cup red wine
1 teaspoon salt
1 teaspoon sugar
¼ teaspoon pepper

Trim excess fat from the beef. Put all of the ingredients in an ovenproof dish. Cover tight with a lid or foil held in place with rubber bands. Steam in a 300° oven for 2 hours until the beef is tender. Adjust seasoning.

SERVES 6 TO 8

CUBED BEEF WITH MUSHROOMS

½ pound fresh mushrooms or
  15 dried
2½ pounds lean beef, cut into
  1-inch cubes

1 small onion, chopped fine
2 tablespoons red wine
1½ teaspoons salt
Pinch sugar

If using dried mushrooms, soak them for 30 minutes in water to cover; discard tough stems. Cut each mushroom into several pieces. Place the beef in a bowl and add the remaining ingredients, using 1 teaspoon of the salt. Steam for 40 minutes. Add the mushrooms and ½ cup of the soaking liquid or water. Steam 20 minutes. Sprinkle with remaining salt. Serve in the bowl.

SERVES 6

GOULASH

---

3 pounds beef (chuck or
   round), cut into 1-inch cubes
2 tablespoons flour
2 teaspoons salt
¼ teaspoon pepper
3 tablespoons butter or
   shortening

3 medium onions, sliced
2 tablespoons paprika
1 cup beef broth or water
¼ to ½ cup sour cream

Dust the meat with flour, salt, and pepper. Brown thoroughly in the butter or shortening in a heavy pot, turning to brown evenly. Add the onions and brown. Sprinkle with paprika and remaining flour and add the broth or water. Cover tight and steam about 1½ hours until the meat is very tender. Stir in the sour cream just before serving.

SERVES 6

GROUND BEEF

2½ pounds lean ground beef
1 teaspoon salt
½ teaspoon pepper
3 scallions, chopped

½ pound mushrooms, sliced
   (optional)
1 tablespoon oil

Place the beef in a bowl and sprinkle with ½ teaspoon of the salt and the pepper. Scatter the scallions and, if you wish, mushrooms over, add remaining salt and the oil, and steam for 15 to 20 minutes.

SERVES 6

MEAT BALLS WITH GINGER

1½ pounds ground beef
1 tablespoon minced ginger
1 teaspoon minced onion
1 tablespoon cornstarch

1 teaspoon salt
¼ teaspoon pepper
1 egg
2 tablespoons beef broth

Mix the beef, ginger, onion, cornstarch, salt, and pepper thoroughly. Beat the egg into the broth and stir into the mixture until all the moisture is absorbed. You may do this with your hands. Form into small balls. If your hands get sticky, wet them with cold water. Steam for 15 minutes. You may do this on a small platter or plate or shallow bowl if you have one that will fit into your steamer, or make a bowl of foil. Be sure the boiling water does not hit the meat balls. Serve in the container they were steamed in or on a hot platter.

SERVES 4

BEEF BALLS IN RICE

1½ cups rice
2 pounds ground lean beef
3 scallions, minced
1 teaspoon Worcestershire sauce
1 tablespoon catsup

1 tablespoon cornstarch
1 egg, beaten
1 teaspoon salt
½ teaspoon pepper

Wash the rice under running cold water until the water runs clear; set aside. Combine the beef and scallions. Mix the Worcestershire sauce, catsup, and cornstarch; stir in the remaining ingredients. Add to the meat and form into balls the size of a large walnut. Spread the rice out and roll the meat balls in it to coat on all sides. Spread the balls out on a wire rack or on a platter and steam for 25 minutes. Serve on the platter or if cooked on a rack transfer to a warm serving dish.

SERVES 6

CHILI SPECIAL

4 slices bacon
1½ pounds ground beef
2 medium onions, chopped
1 clove garlic, minced
2 carrots, chopped
1 green pepper, chopped
2 tablespoons chili powder

1 teaspoon salt
1 (16-ounce) can tomato sauce
1 cup consommé or broth
1 tablespoon Worcestershire
  sauce
2 (1-pound) cans kidney beans,
  drained

Fry the bacon, remove, and set aside. Brown the beef and onions in bacon drippings. Add the garlic, carrots, and green pepper and toss in the fat. Add the chili powder, salt, tomato sauce, broth, and Worcestershire sauce. Cover and steam for 60 minutes. Add the beans, cover, and steam only long enough to heat the beans. Stir and adjust seasoning. Sprinkle the crisp bacon over the top.

SERVES 6

CHILI CON CARNE

2 pounds ground beef
2 large onions, coarsely chopped
1 green pepper, chopped
1/4 cup salad oil or shortening
2 teaspoons salt
1 teaspoon sugar
2 to 3 tablespoons chili powder

1 (1-pound 13-ounce) can
  tomatoes
2 tablespoons red wine or wine
  vinegar
3 (1-pound 4-ounce) cans red
  kidney beans

Brown the meat, onions, and green pepper in oil or shortening in a heavy pot. Add the remaining ingredients except the beans, using 2 tablespoons chili powder. Cover and steam for an hour. Add the kidney beans, stir, cover, and steam 10 minutes. Adjust seasoning, adding more chili powder and salt to taste.

SERVES 8

BEEF-STUFFED SQUASH

2 pounds large pattypan squash
  (pale green with scalloped
  edges)
1 medium onion, chopped
2 tablespoons butter
1 pound ground beef

1 cup fresh bread crumbs
1 tablespoon minced parsley
1 teaspoon salt
½ teaspoon pepper
½ teaspoon basil

Cut the tops off the squash in a circular piece and scoop out most of the seeds, using a spoon. Sauté the onion in butter until soft. Add the beef and cook and stir until browned. Add the bread crumbs. Stir in the parsley and seasonings. Fill the squash, piling up the filling, and put the tops on. Steam for about 20 minutes on a rack.

SERVES 6

SMOKED TONGUE IN A PRESSURE COOKER

1 smoked tongue, 3 to 4 pounds
Peppercorns
1 medium onion, cut up

2 cloves
2 bay leaves

Place the tongue on the rack of the cooler. Add the remaining ingredients and 2 cups of water. Steam at 15 pounds for about an hour. Let cool slowly. Peel and trim the tongue. Serve hot or cold with raisin or horseradish sauce if you wish.

SERVES 4 TO 6

FRESH TONGUE IN A PRESSURE COOKER

Proceed as for Smoked Tongue in a Pressure Cooker,* adding 2 teaspoons salt to the water. It may not be necessary to peel the tongue. Test for doneness after 40 minutes. Trim any excess fat. Reheat.

SERVES 4 TO 6

CORNED BEEF IN A PRESSURE COOKER

1 3½-pound piece lean corned beef
1 clove garlic, slivered (optional)

1 bay leaf, crushed
Few crushed peppercorns

Wash the beef. Make slits with the point of a knife and insert pieces of garlic. Place in a pressure cooker with 2 cups of water and the bay leaf and pepper. Steam at 15 pounds for about 45 minutes. Cool slowly. You may omit garlic if you wish.

SERVES 6

CORNED BEEF AND CABBAGE

1 3½-pound piece of lean
  corned beef
1 large head cabbage

6 medium large potatoes
6 medium carrots (optional)
Melted butter

If not using mild-cured corned beef, soak it for several hours in cold water, changing the water two or three times. Place the corned beef on the rack of a steamer and steam for 3 hours. Replace water in the bottom as it boils away; watch it. Meanwhile, cut the cabbage into six wedges, peel the potatoes, and scrape and trim the carrots if you decide to use them. After 2⅓ hours, add the potatoes, and 20 minutes later, the cabbage and carrots. If you have a multilayered steamer, put the corned beef in the bottom, the potatoes in the second tier, and the cabbage and carrots in the top. It can all be done on one rack if you have a large enough steamer. Sprinkle a little melted butter over the vegetables when serving.

SERVES 6

PRESSURE-COOKED ASSORTED MEATS
(Bollito Misto)

About 1 pound each of 3 or 4 meats chosen from beef, ham, veal, corned beef, chicken, calf tongue, and Italian sausage
About 1½ cups beef broth
3 or 4 vegetables chosen from potatoes, whole small onions, carrots, cabbage, and turnips

If necessary, tie the meat so that it will be easy to slice. Put the meats in a pressure cooker with broth; the broth should be about 1 inch deep. Cook at 10 pounds pressure for 20 minutes. Remove the tender meats. Leave the beef if not tender; it depends upon the cut you are using. Place the meats on a heated platter and keep warm. Put the vegetables in the cooker and steam for about 12 minutes. Reduce pressure immediately. Place around the meat. Serve some of the liquid separately. Carve at the table, giving each person the meats and vegetables of his choice.

SERVES 8

VEAL POT ROAST

1 3-pound boneless veal roast
2 tablespoons butter or other
  shortening
1 clove garlic, crushed
  (optional)

1 teaspoon salt
¼ teaspoon pepper
½ teaspoon thyme
1 cup white wine
Flour (optional)

Brown the roast in butter or shortening in a casserole, turning to brown evenly. Add the remaining ingredients, using ½ cup of wine. Cover tight and steam until the veal is tender, about 1½ hours. Watch to make sure the liquid doesn't boil off. Add more wine as necessary. If the cup of wine is not enough, add a little water. Thicken the liquid with a little flour and water paste if you wish.

SERVES 6

VEAL POT ROAST IN A PRESSURE COOKER

1 3½-pound piece of boneless
  veal loin
2 tablespoons olive oil
1 large onion, sliced thin
1 teaspoon salt

¼ teaspoon pepper
3 tablespoons minced parsley
1 cup red or white wine or
  champagne

Brown the meat on all sides in the hot oil in a pressure cooker. Add the onion and cook and stir until limp. Add the remaining ingredients, cover, and steam at 10 pounds for 30 minutes. Let cool gradually. Remove the veal to a warm platter. Strain the juices if you wish, or purée them if the onion is still in pieces. Pour over the veal or serve in a gravy boat. The gravy should not be too thick.

SERVES 6

VEAL WITH TUNA SAUCE
(Vitello Tonnato)

---

1 3½-pound piece of leg of veal
1 onion, cut up
1 carrot, cut up
1 bay leaf
1 teaspoon salt
1 (7-ounce) can tuna packed in oil

1 (4-ounce) can anchovies
⅓ cup olive oil
Juice 1 large lemon
1 (2¼-ounce) bottle capers

If the veal has a bone, have the butcher remove it or do it yourself and tie the veal into an oval piece. Put it into a heavy pot or steamer with about 1½ cups of water, the onion, carrot, bay leaf, and salt. Cover and steam for about 1½ hours until tender. Add more water if needed. Let cool in the pot with the lid on. Then chill. It is easier to slice thin if let stand in the refrigerator a number of hours or overnight. To make the sauce, put the tuna and anchovies in a blender or food processor and process for half a minute. Pour in the oil very slowly while blending. Add the lemon juice. If the sauce seems a little too thick, add a few tablespoons of water from the veal. Add the drained capers and chill. Cut the veal in thin (about ¼-inch) slices and arrange on a cold platter in slightly overlapping slices. Spoon the sauce over the veal. If possible, let stand for about an hour in the refrigerator before serving.

SERVES 6 TO 8

VEAL IN FOIL OR PAPER

2 pounds veal
2 carrots
½ cup minced onion
½ cup canned tomatoes,
    chopped
2 tablespoons white wine

2 tablespoons butter
1 teaspoon salt
¼ teaspoon pepper
1 teaspoon curry
½ cup chopped parsley

Cut the veal into about ¾-inch cubes, removing any gristle or fat. Scrape the carrots and cut into thin rounds. Place the veal and all other ingredients in a bowl and mix thoroughly. Divide among 4 pieces of foil or oiled parchment or waxed paper. Fold shut, securing the ends. Bake at 400° for 40 minutes. Serve in the packages if you wish. If you put the veal onto plates or a platter, pour all juices over.

SERVES 4

VEAL IN WINE IN A PRESSURE COOKER

2½ pounds veal (leg or lean
    shoulder), cut into 1-inch
    cubes
¼ cup butter
1½ tablespoons flour
1 clove garlic, minced

2 onions, chopped fine
1 tablespoon paprika
1 teaspoon salt
¼ teaspoon pepper
1 tablespoon minced parsley
1 cup white wine

Brown the veal in the butter in the cooker. Stir in the flour, garlic, onions, paprika, salt, pepper, and parsley. Cook and stir to coat the veal thoroughly. Pour in the wine and steam at 10 pounds for 10 minutes. Reduce pressure at once. Pour the liquid over the veal on a heated platter.

SERVES 6

VEAL PAPRIKASH IN A PRESSURE COOKER

2 tablespoons butter
2 tablespoons olive oil
2 pounds lean veal (preferably leg), cut in 1-inch cubes
2 cloves garlic, minced
1 medium onion, chopped
1 teaspoon salt

1 tablespoon paprika
1 tablespoon flour
2 tablespoons tomato purée
½ cup chicken broth
½ cup white wine
¾ cup sour cream

Combine the butter and oil in the pressure cooker. Brown the veal, turning to brown evenly. Add the garlic, onion, salt, paprika, and flour. Stir and brown 2 or 3 minutes. Combine the tomato purée, broth, and wine and pour over. Steam at 10 pounds pressure for 10 minutes. Reduce pressure slowly and remove the veal to a deep platter and keep warm. Stir the sour cream slowly into the juices and stir and heat, but do not boil. Add more paprika and salt to taste and pour over the veal.

SERVES 4

OSSO BUCCO

4 veal knuckles or shank bones
2 tablespoons olive oil
1 teaspoon salt
¼ teaspoon pepper

1 large clove garlic, minced
½ cup white wine
¼ cup tomato paste

Choose veal knuckles with quite a bit of meat on them; the pieces should be 2 to 3 inches thick. Brown on all sides in oil in a heavy pot. Add the salt, pepper, and garlic. Combine the wine with tomato paste and pour it over. Cover tight and steam for about 1½ hours until the meat is very tender. Add a little water or more wine if necessary to keep the meat steaming.

SERVES 4

CALF'S LIVER

2 pounds calf's liver, in one
  piece
1 teaspoon salt
½ teaspoon pepper
Pinch thyme

1 tablespoon olive oil or melted
  butter
1 tablespoon grated onion
  (optional)

Place the liver on a piece of foil. Sprinkle with salt, pepper, and thyme. Combine the oil or butter with onion, if you wish, and spread over the liver. Wrap tight and place on the rack of a steamer and steam for half an hour. Remove from heat and let it sit for a few minutes before carving.

SERVES 6

RACK OF LAMB

1 rack of lamb (about 2 to 3
  pounds, 4 to 8 chops)
1 tablespoon olive oil

1 teaspoon salt
½ teaspoon pepper

Have the butcher crack the bones into 4 or 8 chops so you can carve it easily. "French" the chops, cutting away the fat between the bones for about 2 inches from the tips. Also trim any excess fat. Rub with olive oil and sprinkle with salt and pepper. Steam, fat side down, for 10 minutes. Turn and steam 10 minutes more. The lamb should be pink. You may test it with the tip of a sharp knife for doneness if you wish. Carve and serve on warm plates.

SERVES 4 TO 6

LAMB CHOPS OR STEAKS IN FOIL

3 pounds lamb (6 lamb chops,
  4 shoulder chops, or 4 steaks)
½ teaspoon rosemary
1 teaspoon salt
¼ teaspoon pepper
1 large onion, chopped

3 large carrots, scraped and cut
  into strips
1 stalk celery, scraped and diced
4 medium potatoes, peeled and
  sliced

Put each portion of lamb on a square of foil. Sprinkle with rosemary, salt, and pepper. Divide the vegetables among the 4 pieces of foil. Wrap and seal the edges. Bake in a preheated 400° oven for about half an hour. If you want the lamb well done, cook it a few minutes longer. Serve each portion in its foil.

SERVES 4

LAMB SHOULDER

1 5-pound lamb shoulder
2 tablespoons soft butter
1 teaspoon salt

½ teaspoon rosemary or dill
Parsley sprigs

Cut off any excess fat and rub the lamb with butter mixed with salt and rosemary or dill. Place the parsley on the rack of a steamer and place the lamb on top. Cover tight and steam for 1½ hours. Check to see if more water is needed and if the lamb is fork tender. (It should be very tender.) If not, cook another few minutes.

SERVES 8

IRISH VEGETABLE STEW

3½ pounds lamb, cut into
  1-inch cubes (part neck if
  you are Irish)
1 teaspoon salt
¼ teaspoon pepper
2 tablespoons flour
2 tablespoons butter or
  shortening
1 cup water

1 pound carrots, scraped and
  cut up
12 new potatoes, peeled
2 cups cut fresh or 1
  (11-ounce) package frozen
  green beans
2 cups shelled fresh or 1
  (10-ounce) package frozen
  peas

Trim the lamb and sprinkle with a mixture of the salt, pepper, and flour. Brown it in butter or shortening in a heavy pot that has a tight-fitting lid. Add the water slowly while stirring. Cover and steam for 40 minutes. Check the water level and add a little as needed. Add the carrots and potatoes. Steam for 15 minutes. If using fresh beans and peas, add and steam 15 to 20 minutes. If using frozen, thaw before adding and steam for 12 minutes. Serve with the juices.

SERVES 6

IRISH STEW

3 pounds shoulder of lamb, cut
    into 1½-inch cubes
3 large carrots, scraped and cut
    into pieces 3 inches long
12 small white onions, peeled

6 potatoes, peeled and cut up
1½ teaspoons salt
¼ teaspoon pepper
1½ cups water
3 tablespoons flour

Trim excess fat from the lamb. Put on the rack of a steamer, pour in 1 cup of water, and steam for an hour. Add the remaining ingredients except flour. Add more water if needed and steam a little longer. Put the meat on a warm platter and surround with the vegetables. Skim the fat off the liquid and thicken it with a little flour and water paste. Dumplings* are often served in Ireland with this, their national stew.

SERVES 6

LAMB SHANKS

4 lamb shanks
¼ cup flour
1 teaspoon salt
¼ teaspoon pepper

2 tablespoons oil
1 tablespoon butter
1 clove garlic, minced
1 cup chicken broth

Roll the shanks in flour mixed with the salt and pepper. Brown in the oil and butter, turning to brown evenly. Add the garlic and stir a minute. Pour in ½ cup of the broth. Cover and steam for 2 hours until very tender. Add the remaining broth as needed. Remove the shanks and thicken the juices with a little of the remaining seasoned flour made into a paste with a little water. Pour over the lamb. Lamb shanks may be cooked in clay at 400°, adding about 30 minutes to the cooking time.

SERVES 4

WHITE LAMB STEW IN A PRESSURE COOKER
(Blanquette)

1 onion, sliced
1 clove garlic, minced
2 scallions, chopped
1 teaspoon dried rosemary,
   thyme, or basil
1 teaspoon salt
¼ teaspoon pepper

3 pounds lean lamb, cubed
1½ cups white wine
½ cup water
12 small potatoes, peeled
12 white onions, peeled
6 large or 12 small carrots
2 tablespoons flour

Put the onion, garlic, and scallions into a pressure cooker with the herb, salt, pepper, and the lamb. Pour in the wine and water. Cover and steam at 10 pounds pressure for 15 minutes. Reduce the pressure slowly, open, and add the vegetables. If the carrots are large, cut in 2-inch lengths. Cover and bring pressure again to 10 pounds. Steam for 6 minutes. Remove meat and vegetables with a slotted spoon to a warm bowl and keep hot. Thicken the juices with the flour made into a paste with a little water. Boil a minute or two until smooth and thickened. Pour the gravy over the stew.

SERVES 6

LAMB WITH VEGETABLES

2 pounds lean lamb, cut into
   1-inch cubes
1 large onion, chopped
3 large tomatoes, peeled and cut
   up
2 green peppers, seeded and cut
   up

1 medium eggplant, peeled and
   cut up
2 tablespoons olive oil
1 cup red wine or part water
1 teaspoon salt
Pinch sugar
Flour (optional)

Combine all of the ingredients in a bowl. Place in a heatproof dish. Cover and cook in a steamer for 50 minutes until tender. You may put the dish in a 400° oven if you prefer. Be sure the dish is covered tight. Thicken the juices with a little flour and water paste if you wish.

SERVES 4

LAMB WITH YOGURT

2 pounds lean lamb, cut into
  ¾-inch cubes
1 clove garlic, minced
1 onion, grated
16 ounces yogurt

2 tablespoons lemon juice
1 teaspoon salt
¼ teaspoon pepper
1 cup canned or 2 ripe fresh
  tomatoes, peeled and chopped

Combine the lamb with the remaining ingredients and stir thoroughly. Let stand for several hours. Put into a heatproof serving bowl and place in a steamer for 40 minutes.

SERVES 4

LAMB COUSCOUS

½ cup dry or canned
   chick-peas
1½ to 2 pounds lean lamb, cut
   up
3 large onions, cut up
5 tablespoons butter
1 teaspoon salt
½ teaspoon pepper

2 teaspoons sugar
½ teaspoon ginger
½ teaspoon turmeric
1 bunch carrots, scraped and
   cut up
2 cups couscous, washed and
   dried
Flour (optional)

If using dry chick-peas, soak overnight. Change the water and cook for 45 minutes. When cool, rub the skins off; they will float to the top and are easy to scoop off. If using canned peas, just peel them. Put the lamb, about ⅓ of the onions, and 3 tablespoons butter in the bottom of the *couscousière* or pot and brown, turning to brown evenly. Add the salt and spices and a cup of water. Cover and steam 40 minutes. Add the chick-peas, carrots, and remaining onions. Put the couscous on the top rack on a moist cloth and steam for 20 minutes. Remove to a warm platter and toss with remaining butter. Either pile the lamb and vegetables in the center or around the couscous. Thicken the juices with flour if you wish and pour over.

SERVES 4 TO 6

STUFFED GRAPE LEAVES

1 (10-ounce) jar grape leaves
1½ pounds ground raw lamb
1 pound uncooked rice
1 large clove garlic, minced

1 teaspoon salt
¼ teaspoon pepper
½ teaspoon cinnamon
Lemon wedges

Soak the leaves in warm water for a few minutes to make them easier to roll. Combine the remaining ingredients, except lemon wedges, and mix well. Spread out the leaves and put 1 tablespoon of the mixture in the center of each. Roll up from the wide side so the point is on top. Fold in the sides as you roll. Fasten with toothpicks. Don't roll too tight since this filling will expand. Put onto a rack in a steamer or on a piece of cloth or foil on the steamer rack. Steam for about 45 minutes. Serve hot or cold with lemon wedges. Especially good if served as an appetizer or as a first course.

SERVES 8

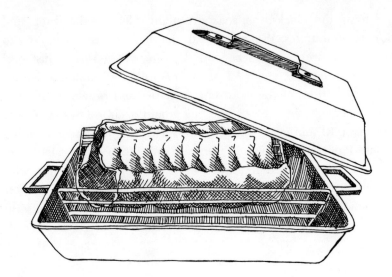

PORK LOIN

1 4½-pound piece of pork leg
  (often called fresh ham)
1 clove garlic, slivered
3 tablespoons prepared mustard

2 tablespoons soy sauce
1 tablespoon sugar, granulated
  or brown

Wipe the pork and pierce with the point of a small sharp knife. Force garlic slivers into the cuts. Combine the remaining ingredients and rub over the pork, letting it seep into the cuts. Steam for 2 hours. This should be moist and not need gravy. However, you can make gravy with beef broth mixed with a little cornstarch or flour and heated with soy sauce and a crushed clove of garlic just before serving. If you want to brown the roast, put the pork into a preheated 450°oven for the last half hour of cooking.

SERVES 8

PORK TENDERLOIN IN SAUCE

1½ pounds pork tenderloin
1 teaspoon salt
¼ teaspoon pepper
½ teaspoon Spanish or other
  mild paprika

1 medium onion, chopped
2 tablespoons butter
½ teaspoon prepared mustard
1 cup chicken or beef broth
½ cup heavy cream

Slice the pork into 1-inch rounds. Place on foil with ½ teaspoon salt, the pepper, and paprika and steam in a 400° oven for 45 minutes. Meanwhile, sauté the onion in butter until limp. Add the mustard, broth, and remaining salt. Simmer for 3 or 4 minutes. Turn the heat off and stir in the cream. Remove the pork from the foil and put into the sauce with any juices. Taste for seasoning and reheat gently. Do not let the sauce boil.

SERVES 4

PORK WITH SHERRY

1 piece of boned pork, 2½ to 3
  pounds
1 tablespoon sugar

½ teaspoon salt
¼ cup sherry

Remove excess fat and steam the pork for an hour in foil or on a platter. Combine the sugar, salt, and sherry and spread half the mixture over the pork. Steam 20 minutes more. Heat the remaining sugar-sherry mixture and pour over the pork after it has been put onto a warm platter.

SERVES 6

PORK CHOPS WITH SAUERKRAUT AND POTATOES IN A PRESSURE COOKER

4 large lean pork chops
1 large onion, sliced
2 tablespoons oil
1 teaspoon salt
½ teaspoon pepper

1 teaspoon sugar
2 pounds sauerkraut
4 large potatoes, peeled
1 cup white wine

Brown the chops and onions in oil in the bottom of a pressure cooker. Season with salt, pepper, and sugar. Wash the sauerkraut thoroughly in very cold water. Drain and add to the pork. Push the potatoes into the sauerkraut. Pour the wine over, cover, and steam at 10 pounds pressure for 15 minutes. Let cool slightly and serve on a hot platter.

SERVES 4

PORK SLICES

2½ pounds lean pork, sliced
   thin
1 teaspoon salt
½ teaspoon pepper

½ teaspoon dry mustard
2 tablespoons sherry or dry
   vermouth

Rub the pork with a mixture of the salt, pepper, and mustard. Sprinkle with sherry or vermouth and steam for 25 minutes on a piece of foil or a plate on one rack of a steamer.

SERVES 6

PORK CHOPS WITH APPLES

6 pork chops, ½ to ¾ inch
    thick
Pork fat or 2 tablespoons oil
1 medium onion, minced
1 teaspoon salt
½ teaspoon pepper

1 tablespoon fresh or ½
    teaspoon dried thyme
1 pound apples, peeled, cored,
    and thickly sliced
1 tablespoon prepared mustard
1 cup beef broth

Trim the excess fat from the pork chops and brown it in a pot. Remove any solid pieces. Brown the chops in the pork fat, or in oil if you prefer, turning to brown evenly. Stir in the onion. Season with salt, pepper, and thyme. Place the apple slices over the chops. Mix the mustard into the broth and pour over all. If using a pressure cooker, cover and steam at 10 pounds pressure for 15 minutes. If using a heavy pot or Dutch oven, cover tight and steam for 35 minutes. For a change, substitute tomato juice for the broth. Remove the chops and apples (the apples will be very soft) to a platter and keep warm. Scoop off as much fat from the juices as you can and pour remaining juices over the chops or serve separately.

SERVES 6

PORK WITH MUSHROOMS

3 cups minced pork
½ pound mushrooms, chopped
  fine
1 scallion, minced

1 tablespoon soy sauce or 1
  teaspoon salt
Pinch sugar
1 teaspoon cornstarch

Combine the pork and mushrooms with scallion. Add the soy sauce or salt, sugar, and cornstarch. Mix thoroughly and place in a bowl. Steam for 30 minutes. You may form into balls if you wish and steam them for 25 minutes.

SERVES 4

PORK WITH VEGETABLES

1½ pounds pork, ground or
  minced
½ teaspoon dry mustard
1 teaspoon salt
¼ teaspoon pepper

2 teaspoons cornstarch
½ cup diced carrots
3 scallions, chopped fine
1 tablespoon minced parsley

Put the pork into a bowl. Mix the mustard, salt, pepper, and cornstarch. Stir into the pork. Form into a flattened mound and steam for 25 minutes in the bowl or on a platter. Stir in the carrots and scallions and steam 15 minutes more. Serve sprinkled with parsley either in the dish it was cooked in or on a warm platter.

SERVES 4

PORK-STUFFED EGGPLANT

1 large eggplant   *½ pound pork, ground*
1½ teaspoons salt   *¼ teaspoon pepper*
½ cup bread crumbs   *1 tablespoon oil*

Cut the eggplant in half lengthwise. Scoop out the seeds and sprinkle the eggplant with ½ teaspoon salt. Combine the crumbs with pork, remaining salt, pepper, and oil. Pile the mixture high into one side of the eggplant and cover with the top half. You may have to tie it on. Steam until tender, about 20 minutes. To serve, cut into slices across the eggplant and stuffing.

SERVES 4

HAM-STUFFED EGGPLANT

Substitute ½ pound minced ham for the pork in Pork-Stuffed Eggplant* and reduce the salt to the ½ teaspoon sprinkled on the eggplant.

SERVES 4

PORK-STUFFED WHOLE CABBAGE

1 large head cabbage
1 large sweet onion, chopped
fine
2 tablespoons butter
½ pound mushrooms, coarsely
chopped

1½ pounds lean cooked pork,
ground or chopped fine
1 cup cooked rice
1½ teaspoons salt
½ teaspoon pepper

Wash the cabbage and cut out the stalk. Boil for a minute or two and drain upside down. This makes the leaves flexible and easier to spread. To make the stuffing, sauté the onion in butter; do not brown. Add the mushrooms and cook 2 minutes. Stir in the rest of the ingredients and mix thoroughly. Place the cabbage on a piece of foil and scoop out the center. Pull the leaves apart gently, beginning from the outside. Fill each leaf with a little stuffing and put the rest in the center, piled up. Tie the head up with string. Fold the foil tight and steam on a rack for about 30 minutes until the cabbage is crisp tender. Remove string and serve cabbage at the table.

SERVES 6

PORK BALLS WITH RICE

1 cup rice
3 scallions, chopped fine
1½ pounds lean pork, ground
1 teaspoon salt
½ teaspoon pepper

2 teaspoons prepared mustard
1 tablespoon vermouth or dry
sherry
2 tablespoons flour

Soak half the rice in cold water for 2 hours or more. Cook the remaining rice for about 10 minutes. Combine the cooked rice with the scallions, pork, and remaining ingredients. Form into small balls. Drain the soaked rice and roll the pork balls in it. Steam for 45 minutes on the rack of a steamer.

SERVES 4

ORIENTAL PORK BALLS

Substitute 2 tablespoons soy sauce for the salt and pepper and 2 tablespoons cornstarch for the flour. Add 2 teaspoons sugar and 1 teaspoon minced fresh ginger and proceed as for Pork Balls.*

PORK BALLS IN RICE

1 cup rice
2 pounds lean pork, ground
1 egg, beaten
1 teaspoon salt

¼ teaspoon pepper
2 teaspoons prepared mustard
1 tablespoon sherry
2 teaspoons cornstarch

Wash the rice and let it soak for 2 to 3 hours in cold water. Combine the pork with the remaining ingredients. Blend well and form into about 40 balls. Spread the rice out and roll the pork balls in the rice. Put on the rack of a steamer or on plates or a pan that will fit into a steamer. There should be a little space between the meat balls. If on plates or pans, cover light with foil. Steam for about 30 minutes.

SERVES 6

BEAN CURD WITH PORK

1½ pounds lean pork, chopped   1 tablespoon sherry or sake
2 scallions, chopped   2 cakes bean curd
2 tablespoons soy sauce

Combine pork with the scallions, add soy sauce and the wine and toss. Cut each cake of bean curd into 6 pieces and fold it into the pork mixture. Bean curd is delicate and will fall apart unless you handle it gently. Steam for 25 minutes.

SERVES 4

PORK AND CHICKEN PACKAGES

1 pound lean pork, diced   1 teaspoon salt
1 pound chicken breasts, diced ½ pound spinach

Combine the pork and chicken. Add the salt. Remove tough stems from the spinach and fold the leaves around heaping table-spoonfuls of the meat. Wrap each spinach package in foil and steam on a rack for 30 minutes. Serve in the foil.

SERVES 4

SPARERIBS

2 pounds spareribs   3 scallions, slivered
1 teaspoon minced garlic   3 tablespoons sugar
1 teaspoon salt   3 tablespoons vinegar

Have the spareribs chopped into 1½-inch pieces. Combine the remaining ingredients and rub them on the spareribs. Let the ribs stand in the marinade for an hour. Steam with the marinade in a dish for about 40 minutes until the meat is tender. You may steam the ribs on the rack of a steamer, basting with the marinade once or twice. When done, heat the remaining marinade and pour over.

SERVES 4 (6 AS AN APPETIZER)

CHOUCROUTE GARNIE

2 cups beer
1 cup water or beef broth
2 cloves garlic, chopped
1 tablespoon caraway seeds
1 pound ham
2 pounds spareribs, cut up
4 potatoes, peeled

6 knockwurst
1 pound Polish or Italian garlic
  sausage
3 pounds sauerkraut, washed
  and fluffed
2 tablespoons gin

Heat the beer and water or broth with garlic and caraway seeds. Put the ham and spareribs on the first rack of a steamer, the sausages and potatoes on the second, and the sauerkraut on the top rack. Steam for about an hour. If you do not have a 3-rack steamer, you may do it all on one, adding the sauerkraut and potatoes for half an hour of steaming. Boil the liquid to reduce, add the gin, and pour a little over all. Serve the rest on the side.

SERVES 6

HAM AND CHICKEN WITH BEAN SPROUTS

½ pound ham, diced
1 chicken breast, diced
1 pint bean sprouts
2 teaspoons soy sauce

½ teaspoon salt
Pinch sugar
1 tablespoon chopped parsley

Combine all of the ingredients and mix thoroughly. Place in a deep platter or bowl and steam for 15 minutes.

SERVES 4

PORK AND HAM PATTIES

½ pound cooked pork, chopped
  fine or ground
½ pound ham, chopped fine or
  ground
3 scallions, chopped fine
1 tablespoon minced parsley

2 tablespoons minced celery
2 tablespoons cornstarch
1 teaspoon Dijon mustard
½ to 1 teaspoon salt
½ teaspoon pepper

If you grind the meat in a food processor, add the scallions and be careful not to make the mixture too fine. Blend in the remaining ingredients. Form into 1½-inch balls and flatten them slightly. Steam for half an hour on rack of a steamer or on a platter. A flavorful ham such as Smithfield is preferable. Add the salt to taste; the amount depends upon the saltiness of the ham.

SERVES 4

JAMBALAYA

2 medium onions, chopped
1½ cups rice
2 tablespoons oil
1 (28-ounce) can tomatoes,
   whole or Italian plum

¾ pound ham, diced
1 green pepper, diced
1 cup beef broth

Put the onion and rice in a pot with the oil. Heat and stir until straw-colored. Add the remaining ingredients, cover, and steam for about 20 minutes until the rice is done. You should not need more moisture if the tomatoes are juicy. Add a little more broth if necessary after 15 minutes of cooking.

SERVES 6

SAUSAGE WITH BEAN CURD

4 sausages, Chinese or pork
2 scallions, chopped
2 cakes fried bean curd

½ teaspoon salt
1 tablespoon soy sauce

Slice the sausages, add the scallions, and place in a bowl. Cut the bean curd into 6 pieces. Add to the sausage with the salt. Sprinkle the soy sauce over the bean curd. Mix the bean curd carefully with the sausage and scallions. Steam for 20 minutes.

SERVES 4

PORK LIVER PÂTÉ

1½ pounds pork liver
½ pound lean pork
¾ pound salt pork
1 tablespoon flour
2 eggs, beaten

1 small onion, minced
1 clove garlic, minced
1 tablespoon minced parsley or
   chives
½ teaspoon oregano (optional)

Combine the liver, pork, and half the salt pork in a processor or food grinder and grind together. Place in a bowl with the remaining ingredients and mix thoroughly. Cut the remaining salt pork into thin slices and line the bottom and the sides of a loaf pan or mold. Fill with the mixture, cover tight, and steam in the oven at 350° for 2 hours. Cool and unmold. Serve cold and slice thinly.

SERVES 8

Vegetables

The flavor and color, as well as the consistency and the nutrition, of steamed vegetables may be a pleasant surprise. Or it may not. You have always been cooking your most appetizing vegetables by steam. You don't boil spinach in water: You steam it in the moisture that clings to the leaves when you wash it. You enjoy green peas cooked in the French manner, with a few lettuce leaves, a pinch each of salt and sugar, a small piece of butter, and NO water. If frozen peas have been thawed, they will cook in 3 or 4 minutes; if still frozen they will take several minutes of steaming after they thaw.

Asparagus is best steamed. Asparagus cookers have been available for years. To use one, place the trimmed, stem end of the asparagus in about 2 inches of water, cover, and steam. If you don't have a pot deep enough, cook the asparagus on a rack over boiling water. Or you may put it in the bottom of a double boiler and invert the top over it. Whatever the utensil, be very careful not to overcook the asparagus.

Artichokes, with the ends cut off, may be placed standing up in a pot with an inch of water and a little vinegar or lemon juice, covered tight, and steamed for about 25 minutes. For a change, use no water, substitute a little oil and lemon juice.

Young green beans and tender carrots take a very few minutes to steam. They keep their original vibrant colors.

The only word of warning necessary is—don't ever overcook.

ARTICHOKES

6 artichokes
½ cup butter
2 tablespoons lemon juice or 1 cup Hollandaise sauce (optional)

Trim off the bottom stem of the artichoke and pull off any small brown leaves. Cut ½ inch off the top with a sharp knife and trim tips off the leaves with scissors. You do not need to trim the artichoke, but it is a little more attractive when trimmed and sometimes the pointed leaves are sharp. Put into a steamer, sitting upright. Steam for about 25 minutes. The artichokes are done when a leaf pulls out easily. Serve with melted butter with the lemon juice added if you wish, or with Hollandaise.

SERVES 6

ASPARAGUS

2 pounds asparagus
1 teaspoon salt
Melted butter

Cut or break off the tough ends of the asparagus. You may scrape the stalks about two thirds of the way up with a vegetable scraper, if you wish. Place the asparagus, standing, tips up, in 2 inches of water. You need a deep narrow pot with a tight-fitting lid. Or you may steam the asparagus on the rack of any steamer. It pays to tie in bunches for ease of serving. Steam until crisp-tender, about 6 minutes. (The time depends upon the thickness of the asparagus stalks.) Serve on a heated platter or plate, sprinkled with salt, and with a little melted or browned butter poured over.

SERVES 4

ORIENTAL ASPARAGUS

Proceed as for Asparagus* but place the stalks in an oval dish and put the dish in a steamer; substitute 1 tablespoon soy sauce for salt if you wish. Steam about 5 minutes.

SERVES 4

GREEN BEANS WITH SHALLOTS

*1½ to 2 pounds young green
  beans
3 tablespoons chopped shallots
2 tablespoons melted butter*

*1 teaspoon lemon juice
1 teaspoon salt
½ teaspoon pepper
¼ teaspoon oregano*

Snip the ends off the beans and place the beans in a low oven-proof dish, such as a *gratin* dish, all lying in one direction. Sprinkle with remaining ingredients. Place on the rack of a steamer and steam for 20 minutes. Serve from the dish they were cooked in.

SERVES 6

BEETS IN A PRESSURE COOKER

2 bunches beets
1 cup water
3 tablespoons butter
1 teaspoon salt

¼ teaspoon pepper
1 tablespoon vinegar (optional)
2 tablespoons brown sugar
  (optional)

Cut the leaves off the beets, leaving about 1 inch of stem attached to the beets. Wash them and place in a pressure cooker with the water. Steam at 15 pounds pressure for 10 to 12 minutes. The time depends on the size of the beets; if very large or if not very fresh, they will take 12 minutes. Remove the beets and, when cool enough to handle, peel them; the skins rub off easily. If small, leave whole, or if large, cut in quarters or slice them. Reheat gently with butter, salt, and pepper. For a change, add vinegar and brown sugar.

SERVES 6

BROCCOLI

---

1 bunch broccoli
1 teaspoon salt
¼ teaspoon pepper
½ teaspoon oregano (optional)

½ clove garlic (optional)
3 tablespoons melted or
*   browned butter*

Trim the ends of the broccoli and scrape the lower part of the stems with a vegetable peeler. Steam on a rack for about 10 minutes or until tender. Place in a warm bowl. Sprinkle with salt and pepper and the oregano if you wish. If you want to use garlic, grate it into the butter. Pour the butter over.

SERVES 4

BROCCOLI WITH MUSHROOMS

2 bunches broccoli
1 pound mushrooms
¼ cup butter

1 tablespoon water
1 teaspoon salt
¼ teaspoon pepper

Trim the broccoli, cutting off the tough stem ends. Peel any stems left on the flowerets. Wipe and slice the mushrooms. Steam the broccoli for about 7 minutes or until tender. If the broccoli is not young it will take a couple of minutes more. Meanwhile, place the mushrooms in a pan with the butter and 1 tablespoon water and the salt and pepper. Cover and let steam for 1 minute; turn the heat off and let mushrooms stand to give their juice, about 5 minutes. Toss the broccoli, mushrooms, and all the liquid from the mushrooms in a heated vegetable dish.

SERVES 8

CABBAGE

1 head cabbage, about 3 pounds
¼ cup butter
Salt

Pepper
Dash nutmeg

Remove the core and any outside tough leaves from the cabbage. Soak for a few minutes in cold water. Shred, not too fine, about ⅜ inch. Place on the rack of a steamer and steam for about 8 to 10 minutes or until crisp-tender. Remove to a warm serving dish, dot with butter, sprinkle with salt, pepper, and nutmeg and toss.

SERVES 6

CABBAGE WITH CARAWAY

2 small heads or 1 large head
   new cabbage
¼ cup melted butter
1 teaspoon salt
¼ teaspoon pepper

¼ teaspoon sugar
1 to 2 tablespoons caraway
   and/or sesame seed
¼ cup water

Cut the cabbage into thick slices or, if heads are small, cut in half or leave whole. Put part of the butter in the bottom of a heavy pot. Add the remaining ingredients, including the remaining butter. Steam for about 15 minutes or until crisp-tender.

SERVES 6

RED-COOKED CHINESE CABBAGE

1 large head Chinese cabbage
3 teaspoons peanut or vegetable
   oil
¼ cup minced onion
2 teaspoons butter

⅓ cup chicken broth
3 tablespoons soy sauce
½ teaspoon pepper
1 teaspoon sugar

Cut the stem out of the cabbage and discard. Cut the cabbage into 1-inch sections. Heat the oil and fry the onions gently for 1 minute. Add the cabbage and turn to coat with oil. Add the remaining ingredients and stir very gently so as not to break up the cabbage. Cover tight and steam for 10 minutes. The number of servings depends upon the size of the cabbage.

SERVES 4 TO 6

CHINESE CABBAGE WITH MUSHROOMS

1 head Chinese cabbage, cut
   into 2-inch pieces
½ pound mushrooms, cut up
2 teaspoons soy sauce

½ teaspoon salt
1 cup chicken or beef broth
1 tablespoon cornstarch

Place the cut Chinese cabbage in a deep bowl with the mushrooms, soy sauce, and salt. Mix a little of the broth with cornstarch and stir into the remaining broth. Pour over the cabbage and steam for 20 minutes. Taste for salt; the amount depends upon the seasoning in the broth. Serve in the bowl or a vegetable dish.

SERVES 6

CARROTS

2 bunches young carrots
1 teaspoon salt

1 teaspoon sugar
Butter (optional)

Scrape the carrots. If some are quite a bit larger than others, split them lengthwise. Sprinkle with salt and sugar and place them in a dish in a steamer. Steam for 15 to 20 minutes until crisp-tender. You may pass melted butter if you wish. Bunches of carrots vary in size.

SERVES 4 TO 6

CARROT STRIPS

2 pounds carrots
2 tablespoons butter
1 teaspoon salt
1 teaspoon sugar

¼ teaspoon pepper
¼ teaspoon minced ginger or
grated orange peel
1 tablespoon orange juice

Scrape the carrots and cut into strips. Put with the butter into an ovenproof dish. Add the salt, sugar, and pepper. Add ginger or orange peel and orange juice. Cover tight with foil and cook in a 400° oven for about 30 minutes, or you may put the dish on the rack of a steamer for 20 minutes.

SERVES 8

GLAZED CARROTS

2 bunches small carrots
Melted butter
1 teaspoon salt

2 tablespoons honey or 2
tablespoons sugar

Scrape the carrots and put them on the rack of a steamer. Steam until tender, not mushy, about 20 minutes. Put in a warm serving bowl, pour the butter over, sprinkle with salt, and add the honey or sugar. Turn to coat on all sides.

SERVES 4 TO 6

CAULIFLOWER

1 large head cauliflower
1 teaspoon salt
Butter

Trim the leaves from the cauliflower and place it on the rack of a steamer. Steam until just cooked, not soft, about 15 minutes, a little longer if it is a really large head. Drain and sprinkle with salt. Serve with melted or browned butter. The size of the cauliflower determines the number of servings.

SERVES 3 TO 6

SAUCES FOR CAULIFLOWER

Cauliflower lends itself to the use of sauces: Hollandaise, buttered crumbs (called Polonaise), garlic butter, herbed butter, or mustard sauce.

CAULIFLOWER PURÉE

1 large head cauliflower
½ teaspoon salt
¼ teaspoon white pepper

3 tablespoons instant mashed potatoes cooked in milk

Steam the cauliflower with salt and pepper for 20 minutes until soft. Cool slightly and break into pieces. Purée in a processor or blender. You may need to add a little half-and-half or milk, especially if using a blender. Add the mashed potatoes. Reheat for 2 minutes. Adjust the seasoning.

SERVES 4 TO 6

CAULIFLOWER PUDDING

1 large head cauliflower
½ cup butter
4 eggs, separated
1 teaspoon salt
4 slices white bread without
crusts

Milk
Bread crumbs or parsley
(optional)

Steam the cauliflower for about 6 minutes, cool and break into flowerets. Cream the butter with egg yolks and salt. Soak the bread in milk, squeeze out, and add to the butter-egg mixture. Fold in the stiffly beaten egg whites. Butter a mold or bowl and dust with bread crumbs. Arrange the cauliflower in the mold and spoon the egg mixture over. Cover and steam for 30 minutes. Unmold and garnish with bread crumbs or parsley if you wish.

SERVES 6

STEAM-ROASTED CORN
ON THE COB

(This may be done in coals or on a grill over charcoal.)

8 ears of corn   *Salt*
Butter   *Pepper*

Pull the husks back and remove the silk from the corn. Push
back most of the husks, removing inner ones; the cob should be
covered with a thin layer. Soak the corn in ice water for a few minutes, wrap each ear in very wet newspaper, and push into the coals

---

near the edge of the fire. Leave it buried for 10 minutes and then turn and cook 5 minutes more. Remove paper and husks and serve with butter, salt, and pepper. You may put the wet paper-wrapped corn on a grill 3 or 4 inches above the coals and let it steam for about 20 minutes. Turn once or twice. Remove paper and always serve with butter, salt, and pepper.

SERVES 4 TO 8

CORN IN THE OVEN

12 ears of corn   Salt
Soft butter   Pepper

Husk the corn and spread each ear with a little soft butter and sprinkle with salt and pepper. Place each ear, or 2 ears, on a piece of foil. Fold around to ensure against leakage. Steam in a preheated 375° oven for 15 minutes. You may put all of the corn on a large sheet of foil and cook it a few minutes longer. It takes a few minutes for heat to penetrate the foil, so even though you cook it 15 minutes the actual steaming is only about 5 minutes, which is ample for corn.

SERVES 6 TO 12

CUCUMBERS IN CREAM SAUCE

3 cucumbers

1 tablespoon butter

1 tablespoon flour

1 teaspoon salt

½ cup water

2 egg yolks

¼ cup milk

1 tablespoon chopped dill

Peel the cucumbers, cut them in quarters lengthwise, and remove some of the large seeds. Cut the pieces in half. Tie them in a piece of cheesecloth or put them in a bowl on the rack of a steamer. Cook for about 20 minutes until tender. Drain. Meanwhile, make the sauce by combining the butter and flour over low heat. Add the salt and stir in the water. Add the egg yolks, beaten with the milk, and the dill. Cook and stir steadily until thickened. Pour the hot sauce over the cucumbers.

SERVES 6

EGGPLANT

2 to 2½ pounds eggplant

¼ cup olive oil

1 teaspoon salt

¼ teaspoon pepper

2 teaspoons lemon juice

Peel the eggplant and cut into cubes or slices. Sauté in a heavy pan in half the oil for 2 to 3 minutes. Transfer to pieces of foil, scraping in all of the oil from the pan. Add the salt, pepper, lemon juice, and remaining oil. Seal. Steam for about 15 minutes.

SERVES 4

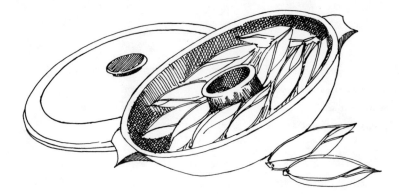

BELGIAN ENDIVE

4 heads endive
2 tablespoons butter
2 tablespoons water or beef
   broth

1 tablespoon lemon juice
1 teaspoon salt

Put the endive and remaining ingredients in a heatproof dish and cover tight. If the vessel doesn't have a lid, put a double piece of foil over it and fasten with a rubber band. Steam over low heat on the rack of a steamer or in a 350° oven for an hour. If using broth, reduce the salt to ½ teaspoon.

SERVES 4

KALE

2 pounds kale
1 clove garlic, minced
1 teaspoon salt
½ teaspoon pepper

½ teaspoon tarragon or
  marjoram
2 tablespoons olive oil

Wash the kale thoroughly and strip the leaves from tough stems. Place the kale on the rack of a steamer or in a colander. Sprinkle with garlic, salt, pepper, and tarragon or marjoram. Steam until crisp-tender, about 20 minutes. If the kale is not young it may take a little longer. Pour the oil over just before serving.

SERVES 6

MUSHROOMS AU NATUREL

1 pound mushrooms
1 teaspoon salt
Pinch oregano

1 clove garlic, crushed, or garlic
  juice or salt (optional)

Trim the ends of the mushrooms. Wipe, do not wash, them. Sprinkle with salt and oregano. Add the garlic if you wish. Place in a bowl or deep platter and steam for 6 or 7 minutes, or put the mushrooms on a piece of foil, fold it shut, and steam on the rack of a steamer for 8 to 10 minutes or in a 350° oven for 15 minutes. Let the mushrooms stand for a few minutes to give their juice.

SERVES 4

MUSHROOMS IN BROTH

Proceed as for Mushrooms au Naturel,* adding 3 tablespoons of strong broth before steaming, omitting the salt. You may use a beef bouillon cube in 3 tablespoons boiling water or, if using consommé, boil to reduce by half. Serve with melted butter if you wish.

SERVES 4

STUFFED MUSHROOMS WITH CHICKEN

1 pound large mushrooms
½ cup minced raw chicken
¼ cup minced ham
2 scallions, minced

2 teaspoons soy sauce or 1
  teaspoon salt
1 tablespoon olive oil

Wipe the mushrooms. Remove the stems from the mushrooms and chop enough of them to make about 3 tablespoons. Place the mushrooms, open side up, on a flat surface. Combine with the remaining ingredients and mix thoroughly. Fill the mushroom caps with the mixture, piling it up and pressing it in place with your fingers. Steam for 15 to 20 minutes. These may be served, with toothpicks as a canapé; they will, however, be cool enough to handle by the time they are served. Also good as a first course.

SERVES 4 TO 6

STUFFED MUSHROOMS
WITH BEEF

---

*1 pound medium to large
  mushrooms*
3 scallions, minced
2 tablespoons butter
1 egg
¾ pound ground beef

1 teaspoon salt
¼ teaspoon pepper
2 tablespoons minced celery
1 tablespoon minced parsley
*1 tablespoon brandy, sherry, or
  red wine*

Wipe the mushrooms. Remove the stems from the mushrooms and chop them. Sauté the scallions for 2 minutes in the butter. Add the mushroom stems and cook 1 minute more while stirring. Wipe the mushroom caps and place open side up on a flat surface. Combine the remaining ingredients with the sautéed scallions and chopped mushroom stems. Put a little of the mixture into each mushroom cap and press into place. Put a little water in a steamer or pot. Place the mushrooms on a rack and steam for about 20 minutes. If you wish to serve them as a canapé, place first on a paper towel to absorb moisture. If on a plate or on toast, you may want to make a sauce. Add 2 teaspoons cornstarch to ½ cup of chicken broth. Stir. Add 1 teaspoon Worcestershire or soy sauce and ½ teaspoon minced garlic. Simmer 2 or 3 minutes until clear and thickened.

SERVES 4 TO 6

STUFFED MUSHROOMS
WITH PORK

1 pound large mushrooms
½ pound lean pork, ground
2 scallions, minced (optional)
1 teaspoon salt
½ teaspoon Dijon mustard

¼ teaspoon pepper
1 tablespoon cornstarch
1 tablespoon brandy or sherry
  (optional)

Wipe the mushrooms and remove the stems. Chop the stems and mix with the remaining ingredients. Stuff the caps; smooth down the stuffing with your fingers, pressing firmly so it won't fall out. Steam the mushrooms for 20 minutes.

SERVES 6 AS A CANAPÉ

OKRA

2½ pounds okra
1 teaspoon salt

¼ teaspoon pepper
¼ cup butter

Trim the ends off the okra. If they are very large, cut them in half. Place on the rack of a steamer and cook about 10 minutes, less if they are very young. Serve dressed with salt, pepper, and butter.

SERVES 8

GREEN PEAS

---

4 pounds green peas   1 teaspoon sugar
Pieces of lettuce   2 tablespoons butter
¾ teaspoon salt

Shell the peas and put on top of the broken-up lettuce leaves, about a cup of them. Add the salt, sugar, and butter. Cover and steam for about 8 minutes or until tender. Old peas will take 10 minutes.

SERVES 6

FRENCH PEAS

---

4 cups shelled peas   ¼ teaspoon pepper
¼ cup butter   ¼ head soft lettuce leaves
½ teaspoon sugar   3 scallions, slivered
1 teaspoon salt

Put the peas in a pot with the remaining ingredients. Cover tight, heat, and let the peas steam in the moisture from the lettuce and butter for about 10 minutes. Don't overcook.

SERVES 6

FROZEN PEAS

1 (10-ounce) package frozen
   small peas
Few shreds of lettuce

2 tablespoons butter
1 teaspoon sugar

Cook the peas as per package instructions, adding the shredded lettuce and substituting butter for the water. Season with sugar. Or you may put the peas while still frozen on a piece of foil, add other ingredients, fold over tight, and steam for 10 minutes, adding no liquid.

SERVES 2 TO 3

FROZEN PEAS WITH LETTUCE

2 scallions, slivered
2 tablespoons butter
1 small head or ½ large head
   soft lettuce

1 teaspoon salt
1 teaspoon sugar
2 (10-ounce) packages frozen
   peas

Put all of the ingredients except the peas in a pot and heat; add the peas. Cover tight and steam for about 10 minutes. If the peas are frozen, cook for 5 minutes after they thaw. Don't overcook.

SERVES 6

NEW POTATOES

---

12 to 18 small new potatoes
3 tablespoons butter
1 teaspoon salt

¼ teaspoon pepper
¼ cup minced parsley

The number of potatoes will depend upon their size. If medium, count on 2 per person; if small, you'll need a few more. Cut a thin strip of skin off around the middle of each potato. Put into a pot with butter, salt, and pepper. Steam for about 20 minutes. After 15 minutes test for doneness with a fork. They should not be mushy. Stir in the parsley and be sure it is coated with butter.

SERVES 6

POTATOES BAKED IN FOIL

The flesh is delicious when the potatoes are baked in foil; however, the skins will be soft rather than crisp. They are steamed, not really baked. Scrub the potatoes, counting on 1 baking potato per person. Wrap in foil and bake at 400° for about 45 minutes. (Sweet potatoes are baked the same way.) They are usually served with butter, salt, and pepper. You may make 2 cross cuts in the top and spread open and insert a pat of butter in each. (This is true for sweets also.) There are any number of sauces to serve with white potatoes: melted butter with crisp bits of bacon, sour cream plain or with a little minced onion and prepared mustard, soft butter or sour cream with minced chives and parsley, grated cheese and a little Worcestershire sauce, cottage cheese with sour cream and chives, or the dressing of your choice. Steam-baked potatoes are the best to use for creamed or hashed brown or in any recipe using warmed-over potatoes.

HERBED BAKING POTATOES

6 baking potatoes
6 teaspoons minced chives
1 tablespoon minced parsley
6 tablespoons soft butter

2 teaspoons salt
½ teaspoon pepper
½ teaspoon dried sage
½ teaspoon dried thyme

Cut a thin slice off the top of each potato the long way and set aside. Scoop out the flesh without breaking through the skin. Put the potato flesh in a bowl. Combine the remaining ingredients and stir into the potatoes. Refill and set the skin piece on top and press in place. Stand on a piece of foil on a pan or cookie sheet. Fold the foil over, being sure to keep the potatoes right side up. Bake for 45 minutes. You may cook these in a clay pot for about 1¼ hours.

SERVES 6

CHARCOAL-STEAMED POTATOES

---

6 baking potatoes   Salt
Butter or sour cream (optional)   Minced chives (optional)

Scrub the potatoes, wrap each in foil, and push them into the edge of a charcoal fire. Cook for 45 minutes, turning once or twice. When ready to serve, open the foil; cut a cross in the top of each potato. Push open, insert a pat of butter or a spoonful of sour cream and sprinkle with salt and chives if you wish. Potatoes may certainly be served plain, letting each guest add butter, sour cream, salt, and chives if he wishes.

SERVES 6

PUMPKIN

---

1 3-pound pumpkin   1 teaspoon salt
1 tablespoon butter or   ¼ teaspoon pepper
  margarine

Peel the pumpkin and cut into strips about 1½ inches wide and 3 inches long. Place on the rack of a steamer and cook for about 20 minutes. Add the butter and steam 10 minutes until fork tender. Season with salt and pepper.

SERVES 4

RICE

1 to 1½ cups rice (preferably long-grain)
2 tablespoons butter

½ teaspoon salt
1½ to 2 cups water

Wash the rice. Rub a pot or skillet with some of the butter. Put the rice, salt, water, and remaining butter in the pot, cover tight, and steam for about 15 minutes. The water should all be absorbed. If the rice is not tender when you crush a grain between your fingers, steam a few minutes more, adding a tablespoon or two of water if necessary. Rake into a warm serving dish with a fork; a spoon will crush some of the grains of rice.

SERVES 4

Variations

Substitute chicken or beef broth for the water in Rice* and omit the salt.

Mushroom Rice. Sauté ¼ pound sliced mushrooms and 1 finely chopped small onion in butter for 2 minutes and stir into the rice before steaming as in Rice.*

CHINESE RICE

1½ cups rice
2 cups cold water

Wash the rice thoroughly in a strainer under running cold water. Put into a saucepan with 2 cups cold water. Bring to a boil, reduce heat, and cook 3 or 4 minutes, total time. Drain and place rice in a bowl on the rack of a steamer. Cover the steamer and steam for 20 minutes. The rice should be tender and the grains loose. When serving, rake the rice with a fork, do not crush the grains with a spoon. You may steam the rice without preboiling by letting it steam for about 40 minutes. Be careful to keep some water in the bottom of the steamer.

SERVES 4

SPINACH

However you are going to serve spinach, on the branch, chopped, puréed, or as a base for poached eggs or fish, it must be steamed first (*not* boiled).

2½ to 3 pounds spinach   *¼ teaspoon pepper*
1 teaspoon salt   *2 tablespoons butter (optional)*

Wash the spinach thoroughly in 2 or 3 changes of water. Remove any coarse stems. Place in a pot with only the water that clings to the leaves. Add salt and pepper, cover, and simmer for a few minutes until wilted. Serve at once with butter or use in other recipes.

SERVES 6

PURÉED SPINACH

2 (10-ounce) packages frozen
   or 2 pounds fresh spinach
2 tablespoons butter
1 teaspoon salt

¼ teaspoon pepper
¼ teaspoon dried rosemary or 1
   clove garlic, minced

Steam the spinach as for Spinach.* If using a blender, do not drain the spinach; if using a food processor, drain some but not all of the liquid off. Add remaining ingredients and purée. Reheat and reseason to taste.

SERVES 4

ITALIAN SPINACH

Substitute olive oil for the butter, add 2 tablespoons grated Parmesan cheese, and use the garlic if you wish but not the rosemary. Proceed as for Spinach* or Puréed Spinach.*

SPINACH WITH BACON

Add 1 tablespoon bacon fat instead of butter. Proceed as for Puréed Spinach,* adding 3 strips of crisp bacon, crumbled.

SPINACH PURÉE WITH SOUR CREAM

Proceed as for Puréed Spinach.* Bring to a boil before adding ½ cup sour cream. Omit the garlic and use ½ teaspoon dried rosemary if you wish. Reheat.

SERVES 4

SPINACH WITH CREAM CHEESE

2 pounds spinach
1 tablespoon minced shallots or
  1 clove garlic, minced

2 tablespoons white wine
4 ounces cream cheese
2 tablespoons cream

Wash the spinach and remove any coarse stems. Steam on the rack of a steamer for 4 or 5 minutes. Drain thoroughly and chop. Heat the shallots or garlic in the wine and add the cream cheese blended with the cream. When the mixture is hot, add the spinach, stir, and serve at once.

SERVES 4

ACORN SQUASH

2 1-pound acorn squash
¾ teaspoon salt

¼ teaspoon pepper
2 tablespoons butter

Cut the squash in half and remove seeds. Put on the rack of a steamer and cook for 20 to 25 minutes until fork tender. Remove carefully to leave juice in the squash. Add salt, pepper, and butter.

SERVES 4

HUBBARD SQUASH
(Winter Squash)

---

2 pounds squash   1 teaspoon salt
4 tablespoons butter   ¼ teaspoon pepper

Cut the squash into serving-size pieces and remove the seeds. Place on the rack of a steamer. Add a little butter and steam for 35 to 45 minutes or until fork tender. Serve seasoned with the salt, pepper, and remaining butter.

SERVES 4

ZUCCHINI WITH PARMESAN

---

3 large or 6 small zucchini   2 tablespoons grated Parmesan
1 teaspoon salt   cheese
3 tablespoons melted butter   2 tablespoons minced parsley

Scrape the zucchini, leaving some of the skin on. Split lengthwise, scrape away a few excess seeds, and cut again lengthwise if they are large. Place on the rack of a steamer, sprinkle with salt and butter, and steam about 10 minutes. You may steam it in a 400° oven for 15 to 20 minutes in foil, if you wish. To serve, transfer to a warm platter or vegetable dish and sprinkle with the cheese and the parsley.

SERVES 6

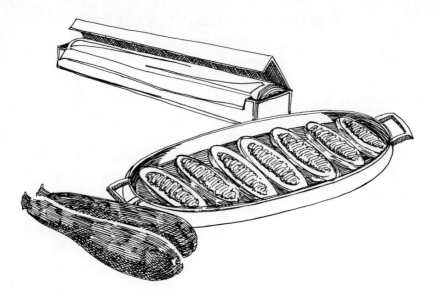

CHICKEN-STUFFED ZUCCHINI

4 medium zucchini
2 cups diced raw chicken
½ teaspoon salt
½ teaspoon pepper
2 teaspoons chopped fresh or ½
* teaspoon dried basil*

1 tablespoon chopped parsley
1 clove garlic, minced
2 teaspoons lemon juice

Wipe and cut the zucchini in half lengthwise; remove most of the seeds. Snip off the ends and place on a flat surface. Combine the remaining ingredients and mix thoroughly. Fill the squash with the mixture. Steam for 25 minutes.

SERVES 8

PORK-STUFFED ZUCCHINI

6 medium zucchini

3 scallions, minced

2 teaspoons vegetable or olive
   oil

1 pound ground pork or pork
   sausage

1½ cups bread crumbs

2 tablespoons minced parsley

Salt

Pepper

½ to 1 teaspoon dried thyme or
   oregano (optional)

Wipe and cut strips off the top of the zucchini lengthwise. Do not peel it. Scoop out most of the seeds to make room for the stuffing. Sauté the scallions in oil. Add the pork or sausage, stirring as you brown it. Add the bread crumbs, parsley, salt, pepper, and the thyme or oregano. If using sausage you will need very little salt and pepper and little or no herb. If using ground pork, use about 1 teaspoon salt and ½ teaspoon each of pepper and herb. Stuff the squash and set the tops on. Steam for about 20 minutes.

SERVES 6

Vegetables cooked on a grill, outdoors or indoors, are a treat. Vegetables that cook quickly and take very little space are well worth trying.

GREEN BEANS ON A GRILL

2 pounds green beans   2 tablespoons butter
1 teaspoon salt   1 tablespoon chopped fresh dill
¼ teaspoon pepper   1 teaspoon minced parsley

Remove the tips from the beans and discard. If small, leave whole; otherwise, slit them lengthwise. Place on a piece of foil with the remaining ingredients. Close foil tight and place on a grill about 4 inches above the coals. Cook for about 20 minutes, turning several times. Serve in the foil, folding up the edges to make it like a bowl. Or you may turn them out onto a warm deep platter or bowl with the juices.

SERVES 6

CORN IN HUSKS ON A GRILL

12 ears corn   Salt
Butter   Pepper

Pull the husks back from the corn and remove the corn silk. Push the husks back and soak in cold water for 10 minutes. Place on a grill and cook for 10 minutes, turning several times. Submerge again in cold water, return to the grill, and cook 10 minutes more, turning once or twice.

SERVES 6 TO 12

ONIONS ON A GRILL

6 large onions, preferably Bermuda, peeled
Soft butter
1½ teaspoons salt

Brush the onions with a small amount of butter. Sprinkle with salt and wrap in foil. Place on a grill and cook for about 30 minutes. Turn several times. If the onions are not very large, reduce the cooking time.

SERVES 6

RED ONIONS ON A GRILL

2 pounds red onions, peeled   ½ teaspoon pepper
1½ teaspoons salt   1 tablespoon butter

Place the onions on a sheet of foil. Add the salt, pepper, and butter. Seal the foil and cook on the grill for about 25 minutes. If the onions are large, cook a little longer. If serving picnic style, wrap each serving in a separate piece of foil with 1 generous teaspoon butter on each.

SERVES 6

GRILL-ROASTED POTATOES

6 baking potatoes
Soft butter or salad oil
  (optional)

1½ teaspoons salt
½ teaspoon pepper

Scrub the potatoes and brush with a very little butter or oil if you wish. Slice lengthwise in half or into 3 pieces. Sprinkle with salt and pepper. Wrap each potato in foil and place on a grill. Cook over coals for about 25 minutes, turning several times.

SERVES 6

FROZEN VEGETABLES ON A GRILL

2 (9- or 10-ounce) packages
  frozen vegetables
1½ teaspoons salt

½ teaspoon pepper
2 tablespoons butter

Open the vegetable packages while still frozen. Put each frozen block on a piece of foil. Add salt, pepper, and butter to each, but *no water*. Wrap them securely and cook on a grill for about 20 to 30 minutes, turning once or twice. You may do the same in a 350° oven. You lose no flavor in this method of cooking.

SERVES 4

CANNED VEGETABLES ON A GRILL

2 (16-ounce) cans vegetables
   such as beans, corn, or peas
½ teaspoon salt

½ teaspoon pepper
½ teaspoon sugar (optional)
1 to 2 tablespoons butter

Open the vegetables and drain off most of the liquid. Season with salt and pepper, and for corn or peas add sugar. Put in the butter and wrap securely in foil. Place on a grill and cook for about 10 minutes, turning over once. The vegetables need only be heated through so the cooking time depends upon the heat of the coals.

SERVES 4 TO 6

Combining vegetables adds interest and variety. They complement each other when steamed together. Invent your own combinations or try some of the following:

GREEN BEANS AND TOMATOES

1 pound young green beans
3 tomatoes, peeled and chopped
1 teaspoon dried or 1
   tablespoon chopped fresh
   basil

½ teaspoon sugar
1 teaspoon salt

Snip the ends off the green beans and discard. Combine the beans with the tomatoes. Season with basil, sugar, and salt. Steam in a bowl for 20 minutes and serve in the same bowl.

SERVES 4

CARROTS AND PEAS

1 pound young or cocktail-size
   carrots, scraped
2 (10-ounce) packages tiny
   frozen peas, thawed
1 teaspoon sugar

1 teaspoon salt
3 tablespoons butter
1 tablespoon minced chives or
   parsley

If the carrots are small, cut them into thin strips; otherwise, dice them. Leave cocktail carrots whole. Place in a bowl and steam 10 minutes. Add the peas, sugar, salt, and butter and steam for 15 minutes. Remove from steamer and stir in the chives or parsley.

SERVES 6

CELERY AND MUSHROOMS

1 bunch celery, scraped
1 pound small mushrooms,
   stems removed

3 tablespoons butter
1 teaspoon salt
½ teaspoon dried oregano

Cut the celery, across the stalk, into ¼-inch slices. Cut the mushrooms in ¼-inch slices; they will be similar in shape to the celery. Place the celery in a bowl and steam 15 minutes. Add the mushrooms, butter, salt, and oregano. Steam 10 minutes. Serve from the bowl.

SERVES 4

PEAS AND SCALLIONS

2½ pounds fresh or 2
    (10-ounce) packages frozen
    peas
Few lettuce leaves

6 scallions, slivered
1 teaspoon sugar
1 teaspoon salt
2 tablespoons butter

Shell the fresh peas or thaw the frozen ones. Put into a bowl on the lettuce leaves and stir in the scallions, sugar, salt, and butter. Steam for 15 minutes. Serve in the bowl to preserve juices.

SERVES 4 TO 6

BELL PEPPERS AND MUSHROOMS

3 sweet peppers (red and/or
    green)
1 pound mushrooms
1 clove garlic, minced, or 1
    teaspoon grated onion

1 teaspoon salt
¼ teaspoon pepper
3 tablespoons melted butter

Remove seeds from the peppers and cut them into strips about 2 inches long. If the mushrooms are small, cut in half through stems and all; if large, quarter them. Place in a steamer with garlic or onion, salt, and pepper. This must be done on the rack in a bowl. Steam for 10 minutes, 15 in clay. Serve with melted butter poured over. Serve in the bowl they were cooked in to preserve the juices.

SERVES 6

SPINACH AND MUSHROOMS

2 pounds fresh or 2 (10-ounce)
  packages frozen spinach
½ pound mushrooms, sliced
  thin

1 clove garlic, crushed
¼ teaspoon dried rosemary
1 teaspoon salt

Wash the spinach thoroughly in cold water and cut off any tough stems. If using frozen, thaw it. (Do not add water.) Place in a bowl or on a piece of foil on a steamer rack with the mushrooms, garlic, rosemary, and salt and steam for 10 minutes.

SERVES 4 TO 6

SUMMER SQUASH AND ITALIAN TOMATOES

1 pound small crookneck or
  summer squash
½ pound Italian plum
  tomatoes

1 clove garlic, minced
½ teaspoon sugar
1 teaspoon salt
3 tablespoons melted butter

Wipe and cut the squash into finger-shaped pieces or into 1-inch rounds. Place with the tomatoes on a piece of cheesecloth on a rack or directly on the rack if the perforations are small. Add the garlic and steam 10 minutes. Transfer to a heated serving bowl. Stir in the remaining ingredients.

SERVES 4

ZUCCHINI AND TOMATOES
IN BUTTER

1½ pounds tomatoes
  (6 medium)
1 pound young small zucchini
¼ cup butter
2 tablespoons water

¼ teaspoon sugar
1 teaspoon salt
¼ teaspoon pepper
1 tablespoon minced chives or
  parsley (optional)

Peel the tomatoes and cut away the stem ends. Wipe and peel the zucchini and cut into 2-inch×½-inch strips. Melt 2 tablespoons of butter in a pot or heatproof casserole. Add the water. Place the tomatoes, standing up, in the pot or casserole and sprinkle with sugar. Put the zucchini next to the tomatoes and sprinkle with the salt and pepper. Add the chives or parsley if you wish. Cover and cook gently for 5 to 6 minutes. Pour remaining melted butter over the vegetables when serving. The vegetables should be tender but not soft.

SERVES 6

THREE-VEGETABLE MEDLEY

If you have a 3-rack bamboo or metal steamer, you can cook 3 different vegetables on racks stacked on one burner. You may serve them in the bamboo. You can manage with 2 layers easily if you have a divided rack, as some new steamers have.

Choose vegetables that suit each other in color as well as taste. Use any ones you like. Here are a few suggestions.

When they are cooked, salt the vegetables lightly and dress with a little melted butter.

CARROTS   BROCCOLI   SNOW PEAS

Scrape the carrots and, if large, split them lengthwise. Steam 15 minutes. Cut off the heavy ends of the broccoli and scrape the rest of the stem. Cut into flowerets and steam for 8 minutes. The snow peas may have to have stem ends removed. Steam for 3 or 4 minutes, depending on size (on top tier if using a 3-tiered steamer) never more than 4 minutes. If they are small and flat, 2 minutes in heavy steam is enough. They must be crisp.

CAULIFLOWER   ZUCCHINI
SWEET RED (OR GREEN) PEPPERS

Trim the stem from the cauliflower; leave whole or break into flowerets. Steam on lowest rack for 8 to 10 minutes, the shorter time for flowerets. If the zucchini is small, cut in half or quarters lengthwise; otherwise, cut into ½-inch rounds. Steam on next rack for 6 to 9 minutes, 6 if in rounds. Remove the seeds from the peppers and cut into ¼-inch strips; steam for 5 minutes.

CELERY   GREEN BEANS
SMALL WHITE ONIONS

Scrape the outer stalks of the celery. If you have hearts, cut in quarters lengthwise; if large bunches, pull stalks apart, wash, and cut them up. Steam for 12 to 15 minutes in the lowest rack. Trim the ends from the beans and steam the beans on the second rack for about 10 minutes, depending upon their size. Put the peeled whole onions on top and steam 9 minutes.

ASPARAGUS   SUMMER SQUASH
CHERRY TOMATOES

Wash the asparagus and break off tough ends. Scrape the stalks up several inches from the lower end. Steam in the lowest rack for 7 to 10 minutes, depending upon the thickness of the stalks. If using crookneck pale yellow squash, wash and cut into quarters or halves; if pattypan, wash and cut into pieces; if they are very small, leave whole. Steam on second rack for 5 to 7 minutes; test for doneness; the age and size of the squash make a great deal of difference. Pull the stems out of the tomatoes, wash, and put on the top rack and steam for 2 minutes *only*.

Bread

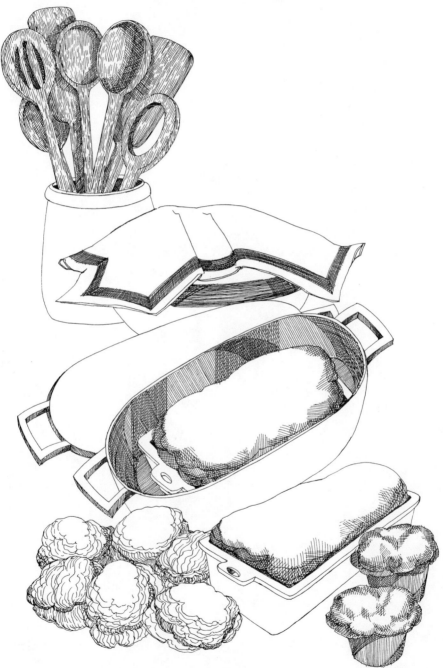

Steamed breads are particularly moist and tender. Fluffy dumplings, light as air, can be produced only by steaming. Chinese buns, stuffed and plain, all come out of the steamer. Baking with steam instead of lighting up the big oven saves energy and it keeps you cool on a hot day. So *do* bake in your steamer.

ROLLS

---

1 cake fresh yeast
2 cups warm water
5 cups flour

1 teaspoon salt
2 teaspoons peanut or vegetable oil

Melt the yeast in the water. Pour this into the flour, stir well, and put onto a floured board. Knead, place in a warm bowl, and let stand to rise at warm room temperature to at least double in size. Roll out into two flat rounds. Brush with oil and roll up. Cut each roll—they should be about 15 inches long—into 10 pieces and place on steamer rack about ½ inch apart. Let stand 15 minutes and steam for 20 minutes.

SERVES 10

DRY YEAST ROLLS

3½ cups flour
1 tablespoon shortening, lard, or butter

2 tablespoons sugar
1 cup warm water
1 teaspoon active dry yeast

Combine 3 cups of the flour and the shortening, working it with your fingers until well blended. Combine sugar with ½ cup warm water and yeast. Stir in the remaining half cup of flour. Pour this into the flour and shortening mixture and work with your hands until blended, adding the remaining warm water slowly. Knead thoroughly. Shape into a loaf or ball and put in a warm place to rise. When doubled in bulk, punch it down and put onto a floured board. Shape into a roll or loaf and let rise again for 20 minutes. Cut into 12 rounds and steam for about 20 minutes.

SERVES 6

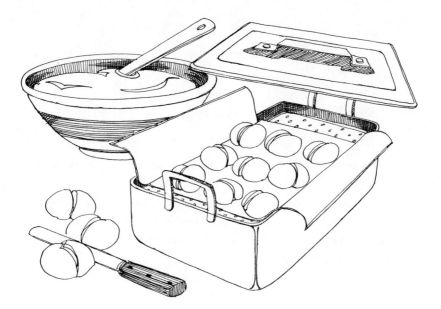

BUNS

---

1 ½ teaspoons active dry yeast
1 cup warm water
1 tablespoon sugar

3 cups flour
2 tablespoons peanut oil
Sesame oil

Mix the yeast with water, stir in the sugar and flour gradually, and add 1 tablespoon peanut oil. Turn out on a floured board and knead until smooth and elastic, adding a little more flour if needed. Knead for 10 minutes. Put the dough into a bowl coated with a little of the remaining oil. Turn to coat with the oil. Cover with a damp towel and let rise to double in bulk—over 2 hours. Punch the dough down and knead for 5 minutes. Roll the dough into 2 logs about 24 inches long. Cut each into 12 pieces. Put each piece cut side down on the same floured board and roll into rounds about 3 inches across. Brush half of each round with a little sesame oil, fold over, pinch the edges together, and score the tops. Place the buns 1 inch apart in a steamer on waxed paper or parchment and let them rise 15 minutes. Steam for about 12 minutes. They should be puffed up. Serve warm on a warmed platter.

SERVES 10

YEAST BUNS

1 *cake fresh yeast*
1 *cup warm water*
3 *cups flour*

Melt the yeast in the water. Put the flour in a bowl, pour in the yeast mixture, and stir. Add a little more warm water if needed. When the dough doesn't stick to the bowl, put onto a floured board and knead. Form into a long roll and cut into 2-inch pieces. Place on a baking sheet about 1 inch apart and let them rise for about an hour. Steam for 20 minutes.

SERVES 6 TO 10

WHOLE WHEAT BUNS

Proceed as for Yeast Buns,* using half whole wheat flour and add 1 tablespoon sugar to the yeast and water.

SESAME BUNS

Proceed as for Yeast Buns,* adding 1 teaspoon sesame seeds to the dough and sprinkling a little over the top before steaming.

SERVES 6 TO 10

GLAZED BUNS

2½ teaspoons active dry yeast   1 teaspoon sugar
1½ cups warm water   Honey
5 cups flour   1 cup sesame seeds (optional)

Put the yeast into a warm bowl and add ½ cup warm water. Stir. Add the flour and sugar and mix well, using your hands. Add the remaining water slowly as you blend. Knead and shape into a ball. If the dough seems too stiff, add a little more warm water. Cover and let rise to double in bulk. Put onto a floured board and knead. Cut or break into pieces and roll into balls. Flatten slightly into rounds about 2 inches across. Add a little warm water to a little honey and brush the tops of the buns. Coat with sesame seeds if you wish and steam for 20 minutes.

SERVES 8 TO 10

PORK-STUFFED BUNS

Proceed as for Yeast Buns* or Glazed Buns,* omitting honey, and, after the dough has risen the first time, divide it into about 18 pieces and roll into flat cakes about 2½ inches across.

1 pound ground cooked pork   2 teaspoons salt
1 pound cabbage, chopped fine   1 tablespoon soy sauce
2 scallions, chopped fine   1 teaspoon oil

If using a food processor, combine the pork, cabbage, and scallions—be careful not to chop too fine. Add the seasonings. Put a tablespoon of the stuffing in each piece of dough, fold the dough in half, and pinch the edges together. Steam for 25 minutes.

SERVES 8 TO 10

NUT-STUFFED BUNS

⅓ cup nuts, chopped fine
½ cup sugar
1 tablespoon shortening

You may use walnuts or almonds or other nuts, or a mixture. Combine nuts, sugar, and shortening. Proceed as for Pork-Stuffed Buns,* putting a teaspoon of the mixture on each piece of dough.

SERVES 8 TO 10

STEAMED BREAD

Follow the directions for Yeast Buns* but after the dough has doubled in size the first time punch it down and knead it. Form into 2 loaves and allow to rise for 15 minutes. Steam for 30 minutes.

YIELDS 2 LOAVES

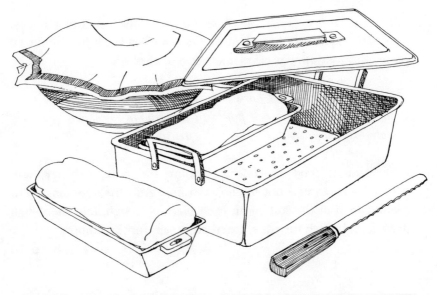

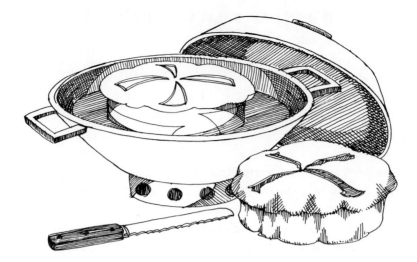

BOSTON BROWN BREAD

1 cup rye flour
1 cup whole wheat flour
1 cup corn meal
½ teaspoon salt

2 teaspoons baking soda
¾ cup molasses
2 cups milk or sour milk

Combine the dry ingredients in a bowl. Stir the molasses into the milk and pour it into the flours. Stir thoroughly. Pour into 3 greased 1-pound cans—coffee cans are good for this—filling the cans no more than two thirds full. Steam for about 2½ to 3 hours, replenishing the water as necessary to keep it partway up the cans. Remove the bread from cans; handle them with a potholder. Cool and slice.

YIELDS 3 LOAVES

GRAHAM BROWN BREAD

½ cup graham flour
½ cup whole wheat flour
½ cup corn meal
½ teaspoon salt

1 teaspoon baking soda
1 cup milk or water
¼ cup molasses

Combine all of the ingredients and beat together thoroughly. Grease 2 1-pound tins or a quart mold. Pour in the mixture so that the cans are not more than three fourths full. Cover tight. Steam on the rack of a steamer for 2½ hours or until a straw comes out clean. Remove at once from cans, using a potholder, and let cool before slicing.

YIELDS 1 OR 2 LOAVES

GRAPENUT BROWN BREAD

1 cup graham flour
2 cups corn meal
1½ cups Grapenuts
1 teaspoon salt

2 cups sour milk or buttermilk
1 teaspoon baking soda
¾ cup molasses

Combine the flour, corn meal, Grapenuts, and salt. Mix the milk with baking soda and molasses. Stir into the dry ingredients and mix well. Pour into 3 1-pound greased cans. Steam for 1½ to 2 hours. Test for doneness with a straw or knife; if it comes out clean, the bread is ready. You may steam this in a 3-pound can if you wish, steaming it for 3½ hours.

YIELDS 3 LOAVES

RAISIN BROWN BREAD

1 cup seedless raisins
1 cup flour
1 cup whole wheat flour
1 cup corn meal
3 tablespoons sugar

1 teaspoon salt
1 teaspoon baking soda
1½ cups sour milk
¾ cup molasses
3 tablespoons melted shortening

Pour boiling water over the raisins and let stand for 15 minutes; drain. Mix the dry ingredients together. Mix the sour milk and molasses and stir into the dry ingredients. Add the shortening. Dust the raisins with flour and stir in. Pour into 3 greased and floured 1-pound cans, filling them no more than three fourths full. Cover tight and steam for 2 hours.

YIELDS 3 LOAVES

NUT BREAD IN A PRESSURE COOKER

2½ cups flour
2 teaspoons baking powder
1 teaspoon salt
½ cup sugar
2 eggs, slightly beaten

1 cup milk
½ cup chopped almonds
¼ cup chopped walnuts or
    pecans
Soft butter

Sift the flour, baking powder, and salt together. Combine the sugar with the eggs. Blend the flour mixture gradually into the eggs, alternating with the milk. Stir in the nuts (you may use assorted nuts of your choice). Pour into a well-buttered 1½-quart mold. Fill not more than three fourths full. Cover with a tight-fitting lid or foil held in place with rubber bands. Place on the rack in a pressure cooker. Put about 2 inches of water in the bottom of the cooker and close the top tight, but do *not* put the pressure valve on top. Keep the water boiling to make steam but not under pressure. Steam for 30 minutes. Take out of pressure cooker. When cool enough to handle, remove from the pan and let cool on a rack.

YIELDS 1 LOAF

SOFT SPOON BREAD IN A PRESSURE COOKER

1 cup corn meal
1 cup boiling water
1 cup half-and-half

1 egg, beaten
2 tablespoons melted butter
Soft butter

Put the corn meal in a bowl and pour the boiling water over it and stir. Add the half-and-half and the egg. Blend well and mix in the melted butter. Butter a heatproof glass or pottery pan generously. Pour in the corn bread batter. Place on the rack of a pressure cooker with 2 inches of water in the bottom. Bring the water to a boil and steam 10 minutes *without* the pressure valve in place. Put on the valve and steam at 5 pounds pressure, no more, for 30 to 40 minutes. The time depends upon how deep the batter is. If 2 inches, 30 minutes is enough; if 3 inches, you need 35 to 40 minutes. Serve in the dish it was baked in, with a spoon.

SERVES 4

DUMPLINGS

(If you are not making your dumplings on a stew)

1 cup flour
2 teaspoons baking powder
½ teaspoon salt

½ teaspoon sugar
⅓ cup milk

Combine the dry ingredients. Stir in the milk, using enough to make a stiff batter. Put it out on a board and flatten it to a thickness of about ½ inch. Cut with a biscuit cutter and steam on a rack for 12 to 14 minutes.

SERVES 4 TO 6

DROP DUMPLINGS

2 cups flour
1 teaspoon salt
1 tablespoon baking powder

1 tablespoon shortening
1 cup milk

Sift the flour with salt and baking powder. Work in the shortening with your hands, a pastry blender, or 2 knives used scissorfashion. Add the milk all at once and mix lightly and quickly with a fork. Drop by spoonfuls on top of any stew or put on a steamer rack and cook about 15 minutes. These are especially good on top of stewed chicken or a veal stew.

SERVES 6 TO 8

DUMPLINGS WITH EGG

1 cup flour
2 teaspoons baking powder
½ teaspoon salt

1 tablespoon butter
1 egg, beaten
¼ to ⅓ cup milk

Sift the dry ingredients together. Cut in the butter and stir in the egg and milk slowly. You may not need all the milk; you want a stiff dough. Roll out to about ½ inch thick and cut into small rounds. Put on the buttered rack of a steamer and steam 10 to 15 minutes.

SERVES 4 TO 6

CORN MEAL DUMPLINGS

½ cup yellow corn meal
1½ cups flour
1 tablespoon baking powder
1 teaspoon salt

⅔ cup milk
3 tablespoons melted butter
1 egg white, stiffly beaten

Sift the dry ingredients together. Stir in the milk and butter. Fold in the egg white. Drop by spoonfuls on any stew. Do not submerge in juice; they should steam. You may steam them on the rack of a steamer but they take on the flavor of a stew if cooked over it. Steam for about 18 minutes.

SERVES 6

CHEESE-CORN MEAL DUMPLINGS

1 cup corn meal
¼ cup flour
1 tablespoon baking powder
½ teaspoon salt

⅓ cup grated Cheddar cheese
2 eggs, slightly beaten
½ cup milk
2 teaspoons melted butter

Sift the dry ingredients together. Stir in the cheese. Stir the eggs into the milk and butter. Pour this slowly into the cheese mixture and stir to make a stiff dough. Drop by tablespoonfuls onto hot boiling meat or chicken stew or broth (about ½ inch apart). Steam for about 12 minutes. They can be done on the rack of a steamer. Test for doneness by inserting a toothpick, a piece of thin metal, or a straw. If it comes out clean, the dumplings are ready.

SERVES 6

WHOLE WHEAT DUMPLINGS

1 cup whole wheat flour   3 tablespoons butter
1 teaspoon salt   ½ cup milk
1 tablespoon baking powder

Sift the dry ingredients together. Cut in the butter and mix with your fingers until the consistency of coarse corn meal. Work in the milk, again using your fingers. Let set for at least half an hour and then drop by tablespoonfuls onto stew or any boiling liquid or onto the rack of a steamer. Steam for 10 to 12 minutes. Test for doneness with a toothpick.

SERVES 4 TO 6

POTATO DUMPLINGS

6 large potatoes, boiled   2 eggs, slightly beaten
1 teaspoon salt   ½ cup flour
¼ teaspoon white pepper

Peel and rice the potatoes. Add the salt and pepper and the eggs. Stir in the flour and beat until light and fluffy. Form into about 18 balls. Drop into stew or put on the rack of a steamer. Keep about a half inch apart to allow for expansion. Steam for 10 to 12 minutes. When a toothpick, straw, or piece of metal comes out clean, they are done. These may be steamed on a stew in a pressure cooker without steam pressure.

SERVES 6

FARINA DUMPLINGS

2 cups milk
2 tablespoons butter
½ teaspoon salt

¾ cup farina or cream of
   wheat
3 eggs, separated

Heat the milk and butter. Stir in the salt and farina or cream of wheat slowly. Stir and cook a few minutes until thickened. Cool. Add the beaten egg yolks. Fold in the stiffly beaten egg whites. Drop by tablespoonfuls into boiling water and steam for 5 minutes. They may be steamed in broth or on top of a stew or fricassee.

SERVES 6

CHEESE DUMPLINGS

1½ cups flour
2 teaspoons baking powder
½ teaspoon salt
⅓ cup shredded Cheddar
   cheese

3 tablespoons lard or butter
¾ cup milk

Combine the dry ingredients and work in the shortening with your fingers or a pastry blender or 2 knives scissor-fashion. Pour in the milk and stir. Drop by spoonfuls on top of a stew or onto the rack of a steamer. Cover and steam 20 minutes.

SERVES 4

SPINACH DUMPLINGS

2 cups flour
1 cup boiling water
6 large spinach leaves or 12 to
    15 small ones, tough stems
    removed

Pinch salt

Sift the flour into a bowl. Pour the water over the spinach in a blender or food processor and let stand for 2 minutes before processing. Add this hot mixture to the flour while stirring. Knead. Put into a warm bowl, cover, and leave for half an hour. Cut off pieces and shape into 1¼-inch balls. Steam on the rack of a steamer for 15 minutes.

SERVES 6

SHORT-CUT BISCUIT DUMPLINGS

Cut 1 can of oven-ready biscuits into quarters. Steam over chicken fricassee or any stew for 10 minutes. They may be steamed on a rack over water but will be less flavorful. You may also make dumplings from a biscuit mix. Add 5 to 6 tablespoons milk and ½ teaspoon salt to 1 cup of the mix. Mix with a fork and steam as above.

SERVES 6

Desserts

You can't make ice cream in a steamer; but you can make delicious puddings and fruits steamed in wine. The magic aroma of festivity associated with dishes out of the steamer is never more potent than when a dessert redolent of "sugar and spice and everything nice" is brought to the table.

PLUM PUDDING

1 cup seedless raisins
¼ cup chopped pitted dates
Grated rind of 1 orange
Grated rind of ½ lemon
1 small apple, peeled and
  chopped
½ cup chopped citron
½ cup orange marmalade
3 tablespoons orange juice
2 eggs
3 tablespoons sugar
½ cup molasses

¾ cup dry bread crumbs
  (unflavored)
½ cup chopped beef suet
½ cup coarsely chopped nuts
1 cup flour
1 teaspoon baking powder
⅛ teaspoon baking soda
½ teaspoon allspice
¼ teaspoon powdered cloves
½ teaspoon cinnamon
Brandy (optional)

Combine the raisins, dates, grated rinds, apple, citron, and marmalade; stir in the orange juice and let stand all day or overnight.
Beat the eggs and beat in the sugar and molasses. Add the bread
crumbs, suet, nuts, and the fruit mixture. Sift the flour, baking
powder, baking soda, and spices together. Stir in and mix well.
Pour into a greased 1½-quart mold or can. Cover and steam about
3½ hours. Don't fill the mold too full. Often served *flambé* with
brandy.

SERVES 8

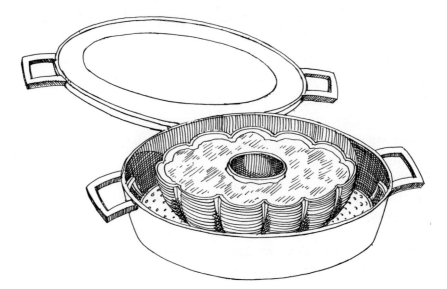

ENGLISH PLUM PUDDING

2 cups seedless raisins
½ cup chopped citron
2 apples, peeled and chopped
½ cup sliced candied cherries
1 cup orange marmalade
½ cup orange juice
Grated rind of 1 orange
1 cup molasses

½ cup sugar
3 eggs, beaten
1½ cups bread crumbs
1½ cups flour
1 teaspoon baking powder
½ teaspoon baking soda
1 teaspoon allspice
1 teaspoon cinnamon

Combine the raisins, citron, apples, and cherries with marmalade, orange juice, and rind and let stand several hours. Add molasses and sugar gradually to the eggs, beating as you add. Stir in the bread crumbs and mix with the fruit mixture. Sift the flour with remaining ingredients and stir in. When blended, pour into a 3-quart or 2 3-pint greased molds or bowls. Fill mold only three fourths full. Cover and steam 3½ hours. Unmold to serve. Traditionally served with hard sauce.

SERVES 12

PLUM PUDDING WITH CURRANTS

1 cup flour
1 teaspoon baking soda
1 teaspoon salt
1 teaspoon cinnamon
½ teaspoon nutmeg
¼ pound seedless raisins
½ pound currants
½ cup minced citron

½ cup cut-up candied orange
   peel
1½ cups bread crumbs
⅓ pound suet, cut up
3 eggs, beaten
⅓ cup currant jelly
Brandy (optional)

Sift the dry ingredients together and put into a large bowl. Mix the remaining ingredients and stir in the flour mixture. Mix thoroughly and pour into a greased 2-quart mold or 2 1-quart cans. Steam for about 3½ hours. Serve hot. Traditionally it is served with hard sauce. It is fun to *flambé* plum pudding for festive occasions. Pour a little (about 2 tablespoons) warm brandy over and ignite.

SERVES 10

RAISIN PUDDING

1 cup brown sugar
¼ pound suet, ground
½ cup milk
2 eggs, beaten
¾ cup flour
1 teaspoon baking soda
2 cups seedless raisins, *plumped*

½ cup candied orange or
   lemon peel
½ cup coarsely chopped citron
½ cup chopped nuts
¼ cup bread crumbs
Brandy (optional)

Combine the sugar, suet, milk, and eggs. Sift the flour and baking soda and mix with the remaining ingredients. Add to the sugar mixture and stir well. Pour into a greased, floured 1½-quart mold or bowl and cover with a lid or foil held in place by a rubber band. Place on the rack of a steamer or in a dish in a deep pot. Steam for 2½ hours. Watch the water level and add more if necessary. Cool slightly to unmold. You may serve with hard sauce or *flambé* with brandy.

SERVES 8

ENGLISH CURRANT SUET PUDDING

2 cups flour
1 cup chopped suet
½ cup sugar
⅛ teaspoon salt

1½ teaspoons baking powder
½ cup currants
About ¼ cup water

Combine the ingredients and stir in enough water to make a stiff dough. Wrap in a piece of cloth or triple thickness of cheesecloth and tie up. Steam on the rack of a steamer for about 2½ hours.

SERVES 4 TO 6

NEW ENGLAND INDIAN PUDDING

⅓ cup sugar
½ cup molasses
1 teaspoon salt
1 teaspoon cinnamon

½ cup corn meal
1 quart milk, scalded
2 tablespoons butter
Vanilla ice cream (optional)

Add the sugar, molasses, salt, cinnamon, and corn meal to the hot milk. Stir and cook until thick. Add the butter. Pour into a mold or baking dish with a tight-fitting lid and steam in the oven at 350° for 3 hours or cook on the rack of a steamer for about 2½ hours. Test for doneness with a knife; the pudding is ready when the knife comes out clean. In New England this is almost always served with vanilla ice cream.

SERVES 6

MOLASSES PUDDING

½ cup butter
½ cup sugar
4 eggs, beaten
¾ cup flour

½ cup milk
1 teaspoon baking soda
1 cup molasses

Cream the butter and sugar. Stir in the eggs. Alternately add the flour and the milk. Mix the baking soda with the molasses and stir in. Pour into a heatproof container, cover, and steam 2 hours.

SERVES 6

ALMOND PUDDING

½ cup butter
1 cup flour
3 egg yolks, slightly beaten
¼ cup ground almonds

⅓ cup sugar
Grated rind of 1 orange
Sauce (*optional*)

Cream the butter until light. Add the flour and stir in the egg yolks. Add the nuts, sugar, and orange rind. Pour into a buttered mold or bowl. Cover and steam for about 45 minutes. Unmold and serve with a sauce if you wish—chocolate, vanilla, zabaglione, or lemon sauce.

SERVES 4 TO 6

FIG PUDDING

1½ cups flour
½ teaspoon baking soda
½ teaspoon salt
½ teaspoon nutmeg
½ cup molasses

½ cup milk
3 tablespoons butter, melted
½ pound figs, cut into small
 pieces

Sift the dry ingredients together. Add the molasses and milk to the butter. Stir in the flour mixture and figs. Pour into a 1-quart mold. Steam for 2 to 2½ hours.

SERVES 6

DATE PUDDING

½ cup sugar
½ cup hot water
2 cups finely chopped dates
2 eggs, beaten

½ cup finely chopped nuts
½ teaspoon cinnamon
1 cup flour

Dissolve the sugar in the hot water. Combine with the remaining ingredients and stir thoroughly. Spoon into a greased 1½-quart ovenproof bowl, cover, and steam for about 1½ hours.

SERVES 6

APPLE PUDDING

1½ pounds apples, peeled and
 sliced thin
¼ cup brown sugar
½ teaspoon cinnamon

Dash nutmeg
About ¾ cup water
2 cups biscuit mix

Sprinkle the apples with sugar, cinnamon, and nutmeg. Add water slowly to the biscuit mix; stir as you add. Put a layer of the biscuit dough in the bottom of a greased mold, cover with apples, and repeat with the last of the dough on top. Cover and steam for an hour. Good with hard sauce or cream.

SERVES 6

BLUEBERRY PUDDING

2½ cups blueberries
1 cup flour
1½ teaspoons baking powder
¾ cup sugar
½ teaspoon salt

½ cup bread crumbs
½ cup lard or other shortening
1 egg
⅔ cup milk

Pick over the berries and set aside. Sift the dry ingredients together and add the bread crumbs. Cut in the shortening until the consistency of corn meal. Beat the egg into the milk and stir in. Add the blueberries and stir gently to mix but do not crush the berries. Pour into 8 custard cups. Don't fill too full. Cover tight with foil held in place with rubber bands. Steam for 65 minutes. Have the water in the steamer not more than a third up the sides of the container. Unmold and serve with a sauce if you wish.

SERVES 8

PRESSURE-COOKER LEMON CUSTARD

3 eggs at room temperature

Pinch of salt

1 cup light cream, scalded

¼ cup superfine sugar

2 tablespoons lemon juice

Butter

Separate the eggs, beat the whites until stiff, and set aside. Stir the yolks with a fork and stir in the hot cream. Blend the sugar and lemon juice and stir in. Fold in the egg whites. Butter 4 custard cups or a heatproof dish and pour the custard in. Work quickly to keep it warm. Have 1½ cups water in the bottom of the pressure cooker preheated. Set the custard on the rack and steam at 5 pounds pressure for 11 to 14 minutes. The larger dish will take a little more time than the individual cups.

SERVES 4

ORANGE PUDDING

4 cups coarsely grated bread
  crumbs

¼ pound suet, ground

½ cup orange juice

2 tablespoons grated orange
  rind

½ cup sugar

1½ cups orange marmalade

1 teaspoon baking soda

3 eggs, beaten

You may use stale bread pulled apart with a fork or the coarsely grated bread crumbs. Mix with the suet. Heat the orange juice, rind, sugar, and marmalade together. Pour over the crumbs and mix thoroughly. Add the baking soda to the eggs and stir into the pudding mixture. Pour into a greased 1½-quart mold or bowl, cover, and steam for 3 hours. Cool slightly to unmold.

SERVES 8

LIGHT ORANGE PUDDING

1 cup milk
¼ cup flour
2 tablespoons butter
4 eggs, separated
¼ cup sugar

1 tablespoon frozen orange
   concentrate or 2 tablespoons
   orange juice
Grated rind of 1 orange

Heat the milk, flour, and butter while stirring until the mixture is smooth and comes to a boil. Set aside. Beat the egg yolks until light and combine with the sugar and orange juice and rind. Add this to the hot mixture and fold in the stiffly beaten egg whites. Steam in a buttered mold or can for half an hour. Set in cold water for a minute and turn out on a warm serving dish.

SERVES 6

ORANGE BALLS

⅓ cup butter
⅓ cup sugar
Pinch salt
2 eggs, beaten
Juice of 2 large oranges

Grated rind of 1 orange
Grated rind of 1 lemon
½ cup flour
1½ teaspoons baking powder

Cream the butter, sugar, and salt together. Stir in the eggs, orange juice, and grated rinds. Sift the flour and baking powder together and stir in. Mix the batter thoroughly and drop by tablespoonfuls into buttered custard cups. Fill the cups only half full, as the batter will rise. Cover with foil held in place with rubber bands. Steam for 40 to 50 minutes. Turn out.

SERVES 6

PRUNE NUT PUDDING

½ cup butter
1 cup sugar
1 cup milk
1 cup bread crumbs

½ pound prunes, cooked and
pitted
1 cup nut meats
2 egg whites, beaten stiff

Cream the butter and sugar. Add the remaining ingredients except the egg whites. Mix well and fold in the egg whites. Pour into a bowl and steam for 1½ hours.

SERVES 6

BREAD PUDDING

1 (1-pound) loaf of white
bread
¼ cup butter
1 cup sugar
3 eggs, separated

⅓ cup seedless raisins
½ teaspoon cinnamon
¼ teaspoon nutmeg
Juice of 1 lemon
Grated rind of ½ lemon

Soak the bread in water and drain. Cream the butter and sugar together and stir in the egg yolks and remaining ingredients, except egg whites. Combine with the squeezed-out, broken-up bread. Beat the egg whites until stiff and fold in. Pour into a greased mold and steam for about 1½ hours. Serve warm.

SERVES 8

BROWN BETTY IN A PRESSURE COOKER

1½ cups bread crumbs
⅓ cup sugar
½ teaspoon cinnamon
¼ teaspoon nutmeg

Juice and grated rind of 1 lemon
4 medium apples, peeled, cored,
  and sliced
¼ cup melted butter

Combine the bread crumbs with the sugar, cinnamon, nutmeg, and lemon. Make alternate layers of apples and the bread crumb mixture in a heatproof bowl. Pour the melted butter over. Cover the bowl with foil and place on the rack of the cooker. Pour 1 cup of water in the bottom of the cooker and steam at 15 pounds for 12 minutes. Cool at once. Serve warm, with or without hard sauce.

SERVES 4 TO 6

CHOCOLATE PUDDING

2 ounces semisweet chocolate
¼ cup sugar
1 egg, beaten
1 tablespoon soft butter
1 cup flour

1 teaspoon baking powder
2 tablespoons strong coffee
6 tablespoons milk
Sauce (optional)

Melt the chocolate and cool slightly. Add the sugar to the egg while beating. Add the chocolate and the butter. Sift the flour and baking powder. Pour the coffee into the milk. Add this alternately with the chocolate mixture to the flour, beating as you add. Pour into a greased 1-quart mold or bowl, cover, and steam for 1½ hours. Serve if you wish with hard sauce, cream sauce, vanilla sauce, or with ice cream.

SERVES 4 TO 6

CHESTNUT CHOCOLATE PUDDING

1 pound chestnuts, peeled
1 cup sugar
¼ cup butter

4 eggs, separated
3 tablespoons cocoa or grated
    bitter chocolate

The easiest way to peel chestnuts is to score them in a cross with a sharp knife and bake them for about 10 minutes at 350°. The skins should curl back from the nuts, which facilitates peeling. Put the chestnuts with ½ cup of the sugar and water to cover in a pan and boil for about 15 minutes or until they are soft. Purée in a blender or processor. Add the remaining sugar, slightly beaten egg yolks, and the cocoa or chocolate. Mix thoroughly and fold in the stiffly beaten egg whites. Pour into a buttered mold, cover, and steam for 40 minutes. Unmold.

SERVES 6

CHOCOLATE SOUFFLÉ PUDDING

3 ounces unsweetened chocolate
¾ cup sugar
1¾ cups milk

1 teaspoon vanilla or almond
    extract
6 eggs, slightly beaten

Melt the chocolate over low heat. Add the sugar, milk, vanilla or almond extract. Do this in the bowl you will steam it in. Beat until smooth. Add the eggs. Beat for several minutes. Cover and steam for 30 minutes without opening.

SERVES 6

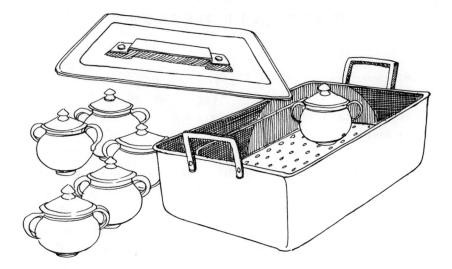

CHOCOLATE MOUSSE

---

4 ounces semisweet chocolate,   3 eggs, beaten
   melted   ¼ cup confectioners' sugar
1 tablespoon freeze-dried coffee   2 tablespoons rum

Combine the melted chocolate with the remaining ingredients. Mix well and pour into *pot de crème* cups, after-dinner coffee cups, or custard cups. Put on a rack and steam for 10 minutes. Stir with a fork and steam again for 5 minutes. Remove the cups, stir the mousse, and chill for several hours. The size of the cup determines the number of servings. This is rich and the portions should be small.

SERVES 4 TO 6

CHOCOLATE DESSERT

4 ounces semisweet chocolate
1 cup milk
1½ cups stale cake crumbs
¼ cup butter

¼ cup sugar
3 eggs, separated
Pinch salt

Melt the chocolate in milk and stir in the cake crumbs. Let stand for half an hour. Cream the butter with sugar and stir in the egg yolks. Add this to the chocolate mixture and mix thoroughly. Beat the egg whites and salt until stiff and fold in. Put into 8 buttered custard cups or a bowl. Cover tight with foil and steam for 40 to 50 minutes; the custard in the bowl will take longer to cook. Turn out onto a hot serving dish or serve in the cups.

SERVES 8

CHINESE CAKE

4 eggs, beaten
¼ cup sugar
2 tablespoons flour
¼ teaspoon almond or vanilla
  extract

2 tablespoons raisins
¼ cup assorted candied fruit,
  such as cherries and orange
  peel

Combine the eggs and sugar. Beat well. Add the flour gradually. Flavor with almond or vanilla extract. Put the fruit in designs on the bottom of 6 greased Pyrex cups. Pour in the batter and steam for 18 to 20 minutes.

SERVES 6

SPONGE CAKE

---

4 eggs, separated
1 cup sugar
1 cup flour

½ teaspoon baking powder
½ teaspoon almond extract

Beat the egg whites until almost stiff; add sugar a tablespoon at a time, beating while adding the sugar. Add the slightly beaten egg yolks and beat for a few minutes. Sift the flour with the baking powder and fold into the mixture. Add the almond extract. Place in a greased pan and steam for about half an hour.

SERVES 6

CUP CAKES

1 cup white wheat flour
1 cup rice flour
1 tablespoon baking powder

¾ cup sugar
¼ teaspoon salt
1 cup milk

Combine the dry ingredients and mix well. Stir in the milk and stir until blended and smooth. Put paper liners in muffin tins and spoon the batter in, filling not more than half full. Steam for about 30 minutes or until a toothpick comes out clean. Remove from tins and serve warm or cold.

YIELDS 12 CUP CAKES   SERVES 6 TO 12

RAISIN ROLL

2 cups flour
1 teaspoon baking powder
¼ cup sugar
¼ cup butter or part
  shortening

1 egg yolk
¾ cup milk
1 cup seedless raisins, plumped

Sift the flour, baking powder, and 1 tablespoon sugar together. Cut in 2 tablespoons butter or shortening. Mix the egg yolk with the milk and stir in. Roll into an oval about ½ inch thick. Spread with the remaining softened butter. Sprinkle with the raisins and remaining sugar. Roll up and place on the rack of a steamer. Steam for 55 minutes. Serve with or without a sauce.

SERVES 6

APPLE ROLL

Proceed as for Raisin Roll,* substituting 3 apples, peeled, cored, and chopped for the raisins. Sprinkle the apples with a little nutmeg added to the sugar.

APPLE AND CRANBERRY POT PIE

3 cups diced, peeled apples
2 cups cranberries
1½ cups sugar
½ cup flour

1½ teaspoons baking powder
1 tablespoon shortening
½ cup milk

Simmer the apples, cranberries, and sugar for a few minutes to make a firm sauce. Use a heatproof serving dish. Combine the flour and baking powder. Work in the shortening with your fingers and pour in the milk slowly while stirring. Roll out the dough to a circle a little larger than the dish the fruit is in. Place on top of the fruit, cover, and steam for half an hour in a preheated 350° oven. If you want the crust brown, remove the cover and leave in the oven 10 minutes at 450°.

SERVES 4 TO 6

CHERRY POT PIE

Proceed as for Apple and Cranberry Pot Pie,* substituting 1 quart of pitted cherries and 1 cup of sugar for the fruit and sugar.

BLUEBERRY POT PIE

Proceed as for Apple and Cranberry Pot Pie,* substituting 1 quart blueberries and 1 cup sugar for the fruit and sugar.

FOIL-BAKED APPLES

4 large apples (Romes, winesaps, or Northern Spies)
4 to 6 tablespoons sugar

1 teaspoon cinnamon
4 teaspoons butter

Core the apples and cut away about 1½ inches of skin from the top. Place each on a sheet of foil. Sprinkle with a little sugar mixed with cinnamon and put the remaining mixture inside the apples. Add about a teaspoon of butter to each center. Wrap the foil around each apple, sealing it securely. Place on a grill and bake for about half an hour. Apples may be baked this way in a preheated 350° oven. Test for doneness.

SERVES 4

APPLES WITH HONEY

---

6 large apples (Rome,
    MacIntosh, or Golden
    Delicious)

½ cup honey
½ cup chopped nuts
½ teaspoon cinnamon

Peel about an inch of skin off the top of the apples. Core them. If steaming on a plate or pie pan, core all the way through; if on a rack, leave the apples solid at the bottom so the filling will not fall through. Combine the honey and nuts with cinnamon. Fill the holes in the apples with the mixture. Spread a little honey on the peeled top of the apples, using your fingers or a brush. Steam for 25 to 30 minutes until tender.

SERVES 6

APPLES WITH CREAM

6 large Rome or other cooking
  apples
6 teaspoons brown sugar
6 teaspoons butter

6 pinches cinnamon or nutmeg
¼ cup heavy cream
3 tablespoons rum

Cut a little skin away from the top of the apples and core them without going through to the bottom so they will hold the sugar and liquid. Put 1 teaspoon of sugar and one of butter in the center of each apple with a little cinnamon or nutmeg. Place on a steamer rack and steam 15 to 20 minutes. The time depends upon the size of the apples. Combine the cream and rum and divide it among the apples. Steam until soft, about 15 minutes more.

SERVES 6

APPLESAUCE

6 large cooking apples
1½ to 2½ tablespoons brown
  or white sugar

½ teaspoon cinnamon
1 teaspoon lemon juice

Peel, core, and dice the apples. Put them in a bowl with sugar, cinnamon, and lemon juice. Steam for 15 minutes until quite soft. Leave as they are or mash them. Use less sugar if serving with meat or poultry. Serve at room temperature. If for dessert, use the larger quantity of sugar and serve cold.

SERVES 4

FOIL-BAKED BANANAS

4 large bananas
Nutmeg
Brown sugar

1 tablespoon lemon juice
Grated rind of ½ lemon
1 tablespoon rum (optional)

Peel the bananas and place them on a large piece of foil or on 4 small pieces. Sprinkle each with a dash of nutmeg, a little brown sugar, and lemon juice and rind and rum. Wrap the foil around securely. Place on the grill and cook for 10 minutes, turning frequently. For outdoor eating, it is easier to have each banana in its own package.

SERVES 4

PEACHES IN RED WINE

6 large peaches
1 cup red wine
4 tablespoons brown sugar

Place the peaches on the rack of a steamer and steam for 8 to 10 minutes, 10 if the peaches are quite large. Cool and peel. Bring the wine and sugar to a boil and simmer a few minutes. Pour over the peaches. Let stand several hours, turning once or twice. Serve cold.

SERVES 6

HALF PEACHES IN WHITE WINE

6 large peaches
1 cup Sauterne
3 tablespoons sugar

Peel the peaches. This is easy to do if you plunge them into boiling water for half a minute. Cut in half and remove the pits. Place on a steamer rack and steam for about 6 minutes until tender. Simmer the wine and sugar a few minutes until slightly thickened and pour over the peaches. Chill.

SERVES 6

PEARS IN RED WINE

4 large pears (Comice, when
   available, or Anjou)
½ cup red wine

½ cup water
3 tablespoons brown sugar

   Peel the pears, leaving them whole and leaving the stems on. Put the wine in the bottom of the steamer with the water. Place pears on the rack, sprinkle them with sugar, and put the remaining sugar into the wine. Steam for about 10 minutes until tender. Remove pears. Boil the wine to reduce. Taste for sweetness and pour over the pears. Chill if you wish.

SERVES 4

PLUMS

1½ pounds plums, cut in half
2 to 4 tablespoons sugar
Grated rind of 1 lemon

Remove the pits from the plums and place them skin side down on a rack. Fill the centers with sugar and grated lemon rind and steam for about 20 minutes. Cool or chill.

SERVES 4

RHUBARB

---

2 pounds young rhubarb, cut into 1-inch pieces
1¼ cups sugar
1 teaspoon lemon juice

You should have 2½ to 3 cups of rhubarb. Sprinkle with 1 cup sugar and the lemon juice. Steam for 20 minutes. Add the remaining sugar and steam 10 minutes more until tender. Chill. Serve from the dish it was steamed in or, if steamed on the rack, remove carefully with a spatula so the pieces keep their shape.

SERVES 4

Index